Reviews for
Becomin...

"Rick Clendenen has made Abra[...]aham, a man subject to the weaknesses and pro[...]s a friend to God and the father of many na[...]ris book is interesting, informative, and inspirational and I highly recommend it to all who would like to become a friend to God."

Dr. J. T. Parish
Founding Pastor—Christian Fellowship Church

"Rick Clendenen has done it yet again. His first book, *Mentoring From The Mountaintop* stirred our hearts. His second book, *Playing From The Second Chair* stirred our intellect. In his third book, *Becoming a Friend of God*, he blends the two; it is the best of both worlds-the heart and intellect meet. Rick's fresh insights on the life of Abraham will inspire your faith, deepen your understanding, and equip you to become a friend of God."

Tina R. Nelson
Intercessor

"I have enjoyed this book tremendously. If I were going to witness to a person of other religions, I would want to have *Becoming a Friend of God* with me. It reveals truth and substantiates it with Scripture. It connects Abraham and Christ, leaving NO room for doubt."

Alan Bray
Business Leader and Teacher

"My friend, Rick is one of my favorite teachers so it was no surprise that his new book on Abraham blessed my life. The way he relives the story makes you a part of the process and his concepts on the development of Abraham's faith are excellent. Your own faith will be strengthened as you follow God's work in Abraham's life."

Rev. Dale Yerton
International Missionary, Apostle, and Teacher

RICK CLENDENEN

Becoming a Friend of God

FIRST STEPS PUBLISHING

Published in 2013 by Richard D. Clendenen, Sr.

ISBN # (will input from Create Space)

Order additional copies of this book and other resources by Rick Clendenen online at: www.rcminc.org

or contact Rick Clendenen at

Rick Clendenen Ministries
PO Box 287
Benton, KY 42025
Office: (606) 848-1495

Cover Art: "Abraham's Prayer", used by permission by Bonnie Joy Kelley
Cover design by Suzanne Fyhrie Parrott
Formatted for Publication by First Steps Self-Publishing Services

Dedication

Life is filled with opportunities to develop meaningful relationships as we encounter new people on a daily basis, each person a potential new friend. It is said that even if you are an introvert, you will encounter more than 10,000 people in the course of a normal lifetime. Obviously, if you are an extrovert, that number would be significantly higher. Yet it is also said that if you can end life with three lasting friendships, you have lived a rich fulfilling life. The truth of the matter is simple: friendships come and go as life unfolds with all of its twists and turns. This is not an indictment against human beings concerning our inability to maintain meaningful relationships, but rather a picture of how difficult it is to foster lifelong relationships in an ever changing world where nothing remains constant.

I have been blessed by God to have a friend that has remained my best friend through everything life has thrown my way. Not once have I doubted her love. Her commitment has been unwavering and her support has, without question, been the strength that has enabled me to accomplish the victories I've been able to attain. She's not only my best friend, she's my wife, my business partner, my personal secretary, my trusted advisor and the list goes on and on. By the way, did I mention that she's the mother of my two wonderful children, Richie and Renee, and the grandmother of my darling grandchildren?

Yes, I dedicate this book to Debbie Peal Clendenen, the love of my life. And I also dedicate my life to support you in every endeavor you pursue until death shall separate us. I love you and this one is for you!

ACKNOWLEDGMENTS

"Success is always carried on the back of sacrifice." Though often unseen, every victory comes with a price. Someone must be willing to pay it simply because they believe the blessing is worth the burden they shoulder. Thankfully, I have been blessed with just such a team of people who have surrounded me because they believed in me, and they were willing to show their commitment through their sacrifices.

Leading this charge is my wife and family who were willing to pay the price of my absence, enabling me to dedicate hundreds of hours to the research and writing of this manuscript. And of course, there are editors, proofreaders, graphic designers, printers, publishers and a host of people that comprise the team that have worked to make my dream a reality. To all of them I say, "Thank you from the bottom of my heart." And of course there are those that have invested financially in this endeavor. To you I am forever indebted.

One person in particular has been invaluable in the production of this book: my agent, Dr. Jose Bonilla who has worked tirelessly to negotiate on my behalf every hurdle that has stood in our way. He has been the person I could depend on to turn stumbling blocks into stepping stones on the pathway to success. Thank you, Jose, for not only being my agent but above all else, being my friend.

Today we present the collaborate effort of this team with our prayer that it will be a blessing to you as you explore your friendship with God.

Contents

Becoming a Friend of God

Introduction

The word *friend* comes from two Old English words: *freo*, meaning free; and *freon*, meaning to love. So, a friend is free to love; therefore, friendships are voluntary relationships that cannot be manipulated. Webster goes on to define a friend as: (1) One attached by true affection; (2) One that is not hostile; (3) One that shows favor or promotes; (4) A favored companion; and (5) An advocate for adversity. The Bible simply states it this way: "A friend loveth at all times and a brother is born for adversity." (Proverbs 17:17)

True friends are friends in the good times and in the bad. As I pen these words, I'm experiencing a difficult season in my life and ministry. After thirty-five years of active ministry, I've been sidelined by sickness, which according to the doctors could take months or even years to recover from. But I must admit, never have I come to appreciate my friends more than I do right now. For I have realized the truth of this scripture, that friends are not changed by the circumstances of our everyday lives. They are not over-impressed by our triumph, nor are they depressed by our tragedies. They remain steady through the battles we face.

So it was in the life of Abraham. Through his victories as well as his failures he was known as a friend of God. And scripture tells us that God was not ashamed to be called his God. This whole story reminds me of an experience I had a number of years ago in a tiny village in northern Kenya on the Ugandan border. I spent three weeks in a village hut. When I arrived, the first order of business was to meet everyone in the village. My friend took me by the hand and led me from hut to hut, holding my hand as I would hold the hand of my wife with our fingers intertwined.

I must admit that I felt uncomfortable holding his hand for almost an hour. When we came back to his home, he released my sweaty hand and began to explain their custom. He said, "I held your hand because I want everyone I'm acquainted with to know that I am not ashamed to be attached to you; for you are my friend. Do you understand now?" I was truly overwhelmed by his display of love.

As you read this book you are going to discover that Abraham was not perfect. Nor were the decisions he made, but God never let go of his hand until he achieved the destiny He had planned for his life. There is much to learn from his journey that will enable us to be known as a friend of God. But our journey must begin with the understanding that God has already initiated this friendship with us. Proverbs 18:24 declares that, "A man that hath friends must shew himself friendly; and there is a friend that sticketh closer than a brother." Jesus is that friend, revealing God's intention to become friends with all of us.

John 15:13-15 says, "[13]Greater love hath no man than this, that a man lay down his life for his friends. [14]Ye are my friends, if ye do whatsoever I command you. [15]Henceforth I call you no more servants, for the servants knoweth not what his lord doeth; but I have called you friends; for all things that I have heard of my Father I have made known unto you." The secret is out: God wants to be your friend! So let's take this journey with Abraham and discover together the secrets of becoming a friend of God.

By the way, let me explain that this book is a work of historical fiction. Although the events truly happened in the life of Abraham, I have taken great liberty in expressing Abraham's feelings based on the way I might have responded had I been in Abraham's position today. I encourage you to do the same as you read the pages that follow. Happy traveling!

Chapter One

Abram the Chosen One

John 15:16-"Ye have not chosen me, but I have chosen you, and ordained you, that ye should go and bring forth fruit, and that your fruit should remain: that whatsoever ye shall ask of the Father in my name, he may give it you."

Imagine the gut-wrenching feeling of standing in line on the playground somewhere listening for your name to be called by a newly elected captain. You have only one desire: to be a part of the team. With every name called and every point of the finger, despair grips your heart while a knot forms in the pit of your stomach; all you can think about is, "Does anyone want me? Will I ever make the team? Will I suffer rejection? How long will this misery last?" It finally ends as quickly as it began when you hear your name break the awkward silence.

This, my friend, was the life of Abram, raised in a culture where barrenness was considered to be a curse from God. For seventy-five years, he carried the name Abram, meaning *father*, though he had no children. How cruel that every time he heard his name called, he was reminded of his curse, his inability to have a child. With every passing year, the feeling grew worse and worse and the chance of living up to his name seemed less and less likely. Finally, all hope was gone; he had grown accustomed to the idea that he was a failure, and nothing positive would ever come from his miserable life. He had learned to live with his rejection.

But in the moment of deepest despair, Abram encountered God who put His finger directly on the sore spot, Abram's name. God not only called his name, reminding him of his failures of the past, but He then changed his name, reminding him of the possibilities of the future. In one encounter, he went from Abram, meaning *father*, to Abraham, meaning *a father of a multitude*. Yet there was not one child to substantiate the change. It almost appeared to add insult to injury as Abraham told the story of his God-encounter and reintroduced himself with his newly given name. You could almost hear the muffled giggles and feel the condescending gazes of the crowd as they mumbled to themselves, "Yeah, right! The father of a multitude! Where is the evidence? All we have is the word of this old man who has apparently spent too much time in the desert heat." But what they did not understand is the fact that neither his name nor his newly declared future had anything to do with the word of Abraham; it all hinged on the word of an all-powerful God that could not lie. And so does your future as well, I might add.

There are many things we must remember concerning God encounters, the greatest of which is that God encounters are God initiated. You don't choose God, He has chosen you. According to Galatians 3:28, that choice was not based on your ethnicity, since both Jews and Greeks qualified. In fact, God is assembling a group from every kindred, tribe, and tongue. That choice was also not based on your social status since both bond and free stand side by side on equal ground. For around the cross, the ground is level. Last, but certainly not least, the choice is not based on your gender since male and female are both chosen to participate. The idea that God would ignore the gender of those He chooses goes directly against many of the world's cultures which consider men superior to women. Yet God has grouped us together and called us all His sons. So here we are, all a part of the same team, regardless of our ethnicity, our social status or our gender, wondering how we arrived and asking ourselves, "Pray tell, what is the criterion for selection?" This brings us to our second principle to remember concerning God encounters.

God encounters are always based on His love: "For God so loved the world, that he gave his only begotten Son, that whosoever believeth in him should not perish, but have everlasting life." (John 3:16) "But God commendeth his love toward us, in that, while we were yet sinners, Christ died for us." (Romans 5:8) These two scriptures go directly against everything we have ever known or believed. For in our world, we know nothing concerning the concept of unconditional love since all of our love is of the responsive kind. Our motto is "Tit for tat; butter for fat; you kill my dog; I'll kill your cat."

How could someone have loved us before we became lovable? The answer is simple: His love is based on His nature and not on our actions. What a comforting thought to consider—nothing I do could make Him love me more and nothing I do could make Him love me less! For His love is perfect love. It cannot be altered because it is unconditional. God did not choose Abraham because he was worthy of the choosing. History tells us that he was an idolater who made idols alongside his father in the family business. Yet, somehow, this flaw did not seem to matter in God's selection process. I must warn you, before you become judgmental, to consider where you were in your own life when you recognized that God was calling you. It is a fact that none of us qualify to receive His mercy and grace. And if we did, it would no longer be mercy and grace; it would become reward and compensation.

Not only are God encounters God initiated and based on His love, they are also centered on His purpose. God chose Abram because He had a plan for his life that was far greater than what Abram could ever have imagined. He was asking for a son but God was offering to give him a nation larger than the sands of the sea or the stars of the Heavens. God's purpose always exceeds our ability to imagine. Scripture tells us that God is able to do exceedingly abundantly above all that we can ask or think according to the power that worketh in us. He would not only father a child but would also be known as the father of the faithful.

We must never forget the words of Jeremiah 29:11 which declare: "For I know the thoughts that I think toward you, saith the Lord, thoughts of peace, and not of evil, to give you an expected end." God is always at work to fulfill His purpose in your life. We know that according to Romans 8:28, "…all things work together for good to them that love God, to them who are the called according to his purpose." Yet there are more pieces to the mysterious puzzle concerning the criteria for God encounters.

The fourth thing to remember is that God encounters reveal His promises. Not only would Abram come to understand the purpose of God, but he would always have the promises of God to hold on to until the purpose of God was realized. We can read these promises in Genesis, chapter 12. These promises not only apply to Abram, they apply to us as his seed. The first is that God promises to direct Abram toward his newfound destiny. God Himself is promising to be the tour guide for him and though he has no idea of his final destination, he can trust God to perform all that He has promised him. Thus is the life of faith born. Proverbs 3:5-6 affirms that same promise to us as it reminds us to "5Trust in the Lord with all thine heart; and lean not unto thine own understanding. 6In all thy ways acknowledge him, and he shall direct thy paths."

God also promised to make him a great nation. Abram had no idea what God had in mind for his life. But the thought that a man who had lived his life under the curse of barrenness would be responsible for birthing a nation must have set him rocking on his heels. Yet God went on to promise to make his name great. That name that had in the past conjured up negative thoughts of failure and rejection would in the future be viewed as anything but repulsive. It birthed in Abram a hope and desire to follow God into his hidden future. That same thing propels us forward as believers today knowing that God has not only laid in store for us a robe and a crown, He has also laid aside a new name and that name will erase the shame of our past.

Next, God promised Abram that he would be a blessing. God is promising to fulfill the greatest desire of every human being, the desire for significance. None of us want our lives to be insignificant or irrelevant. We want our lives to matter and we want to be viewed as a blessing, not as a curse. Next He promised Abram his protection. We find what God said to him in Genesis 12:3, "And I will bless them that bless thee, and curse him that curseth thee...." In other words God is saying, "I will respond to others in proportion to how they will respond to you. And in that alone, I will protect you from the ridicule and assault of the unbeliever."

The last promise, found in the same verse in Genesis 12, is no doubt the one that seals the deal, "....and in thee shall all families of the earth be blessed." Not only would his curse be removed but the curse of every family to come would vanish. Never again would they be exposed to the humiliating feelings that Abram had carried for the last seventy-five years.

For the first time in his life, Abram came face to face with the reality that God encounters have multiplication, and generational impact connected to them. The decision he would make would not only have the potential to change his life dramatically, but it would also set the stage for change in the lives of every generation to follow. You can almost feel the weight of his decision buckling his knees under him. How can I take on this awesome responsibility? What if I fail? Can I do it? All these questions must have raced through his mind one after another.

Now is the time to remember the last thing concerning God encounters: they invoke God's partnership. Jesus said in John 16:23, "….Whatsoever ye shall ask the Father in my name, he will give it you." He went on to promise us that He would never leave us nor forsake us and that He would be with us always even to the end of the earth. (Hebrews 13:5, Matthew 28:20)

Now that God had revealed His love toward Abram, now that Abram understood His plan, now that he had His promises and could rely on His partnership, how was he to respond? For his name was finally being called to join God's team. He could see visions of grandeur as God was offering him an opportunity to hoist a future MVP trophy in the air, to live a life of generational impact and multiplication. Yet Abram was still the one who would have to make the final decision. He would have to put God first in his life, above his family, above his country, above his possessions, above earthly relationship, above his natural inheritance. And he would have to be willing to walk out this plan totally by faith, without any visible evidence to corroborate his decision. Would he make mistakes? Without question! Would he fail along the way? Without a doubt he would! But now it is Abram's turn. God is awaiting his response. Finally Abram says, "Yes" and the journey begins.

Chapter Two

Abram's Bad Decisions

Genesis 12:4-"So Abraham departed, as the Lord had spoken unto him; and Lot went with him: and Abram was seventy and five years old when he departed out of Haran."

I remember as if it were only yesterday although in reality, it was well over thirty years ago. One afternoon I made a decision that it was now time for my son to learn how to walk. For deep inside I knew that he would never be able to fulfill all the dreams and visions I had planned for his life unless he could stand upon his own two feet and move forward. This was my decision and I would have to see it through, but it was a decision based on my best intentions for him. While he, on the other hand, sat there on the floor totally content to live life as usual, surrounded by a support system filled with love where everyone around him was more than willing to retrieve whatever he thought he needed. All the while, he could remain comfortably close to the ground on his hands and knees, away from danger. I knew that though he was comfortable with life as usual, this condition was not conducive for greatness; everything was about to change in his little world, as well as ours. A new journey would begin with his first new step, and today was the day to start.

Of course, I was wise enough to realize that this would be a long process for no one even expected him to walk the first time he tried. I was also prepared to help him cope with his natural fears and struggles as he learned to navigate in a brand new way. And above all, I was fully aware that this journey would be filled with setbacks, injuries, failures and even scars that he might carry the rest of life as a constant reminder of this moment. Yet somehow I knew that the outcome would far outweigh the bumps and bruises he would encounter along the way. I can still recall with clarity the look of fear in his eyes as I stood him on his feet for the first time. With his back firmly against the wall, I knelt down in front of him eye to eye, assuring him that I was totally committed to his success. He could depend on me to pick him up when he fell, to kiss away the pain and to repeat this process however long it may be. I would be his partner for life, his greatest cheerleader. I must admit I was more excited about the journey than he was; maybe it was because I knew more about the freedom we would experience and the possibilities that could now become realities all because he could walk. I found myself frustrated along with him as we worked together, wishing that just once I could allow him to see the world through my eyes. For I knew it would instantly provide the motivation he would need to persevere. I also knew down deep inside that this first step would result in a long walk through life together as father and son. It would allow us to participate together in a variety of activities that would bond our hearts as one. And yes, I knew that someday, many years down the road, he would bow before his own son and he would be able to teach him to follow in our footsteps.

All of these same feelings were resident in the heart of Father God as Abram took his first step toward both becoming a friend to God as well as becoming the father of the faithful. This was indeed his moment in time, fully certain of what he was leaving, yet uncertain of where he was going. The journey began. With his earthly father behind him and his Heavenly Father leading the way, Abram made his first step. No, it was not a pretty sight for he was beginning with shaky legs. In fact, his first decision would ultimately cause him to stumble and fall for he allowed Lot to go with him on a journey to which God had not called Lot, toward a vision that Lot could not see. Such a typical mistake made by almost all of us: we try to convince others to respond with us to a call they have never heard toward a destiny they have never dreamed. It's just a mistake, but Abram will recover to walk again.

In fact, we discover in Genesis 12:1-10 that Abram will make three bad decisions back to back that will land him on his face before God. Yet God would not rescind His call or alter His commitment in any way toward

Abram's future. I noticed, in fact, that none of these mistakes seemed in any way to catch God off guard or to take Him by surprise. It is as if God knew ahead of time the pitfalls to come. And God understood better than Abram that walking by faith and not by sight can increase your chances of stumbling. Yet walking by faith would provide Abram the opportunity to grow personally, while allowing him to impact dramatically the advancement of the Kingdom of God. It would truly be a win-win.

With Lot beside him and God before him, Abram felt as if He were the rope in a great tug of war, caught between his history and his destiny. He felt the tug of both worlds pulling simultaneously, as all of us have felt as we begin our walk of faith. Refusing to leave Lot behind led to a second bad decision. It is found in Genesis 12:8 and, though it is a subtle decision, its impact cannot be overemphasized. "And he (Abram) removed from thence unto a mountain on the east of Bethel, and he pitched his tent, having Bethel on the west, and Hai on the east: and there he builded an altar unto the Lord, and called upon the name of the Lord." The subtlety of this decision is found in the opening statement, "And he (Abram) removed then thence." For in verse six, we discover that God had led Abram to Canaan to the plain of Moreh. But in verse eight, Abram decided to move a little bit away from where God had led him. He will soon come to discover that an inch away from God's will is as damaging as a hundred miles. Why he felt it necessary to wander off on his own is left somewhat to speculation. No doubt, Lot's opinion played a factor but there is also another fact found in verse six: the Canaanites were still in the land. Abram probably thought that God would lead him to a promised land that was free from giants, and having to run the squatters from his possession might have been more than he bargained for. So he decided to move away and camp awhile. The Bible tells us that he camped between Hai and Bethel. It is intriguing to discover the meanings of these two cities' names. Bethel, as we all know, is translated "the house of God" but the meaning of Hai is "the place of ruin." So Abram found himself somewhere between ruin and redemption, between ruin and righteousness, between ruin and relationship, and between ruin and riches. This scenario describes the lives of many who call themselves followers of Christ. They have stopped short of what God has for them and they choose to camp between Bethel and Hai, not exactly a part of the world any longer but not exactly enjoying the fullness that God has to offer them. They're stuck on the fence.

What Abram didn't realize is that many times indecision has repercussions just as decisions do. It is obvious that every decision is a doorway to a new destiny. On the other hand, indecisions seem to open up a floodgate rather than a door that often ushers into your life more and more opportunities for failure by creating a vacuum and a void in your direction and destiny. Simply put, you can't sit still very long before you find yourself going backward instead of forward.

When Abram chose to stop and camp for awhile, stumbling blocks began to surface that would lead to his fall. The first of which was famine. He began to notice that there was just not enough food to go around. Remember this principle: If harvest is the evidence of a fruitful decision, then famine is equally the evidence of an unfruitful choice. I can assure you, according to scripture, that God will meet your needs if you are in the center of His will. But if you choose to move away from His will, then you assume the responsibility for meeting your own needs. That, my friend, is a scary thought, especially if you have invited people to make the journey with you who were never intended to be on the trip.

This is where Abram found himself. Close on the heels of this famine, he experienced the second stumbling block: fear. "How can I do this and why is everyone looking at me to answer their questions and to meet their needs?" he wonders. Once we decide not to decide, fear comes in like a flood to rob us of our peace. Fear does not come from God. In fact, the Bible tells us plainly in 2 Timothy 1:7, "For God hath not given us a spirit of fear; but of power, and of love, and of a sound mind." The phrase "sound mind" actually means "disciplined" or "fixed." Any time we allow indecision to rule, it will ultimately affect our progress as faith gives way to fear.

The combination of famine and fear caused Abram to make another bad decision. He decided to take his family to Egypt in verse ten. Since Egypt means "bondage," it is easy to see that this decision will have lasting impact. For while in Egypt, Abram witnessed firsthand the detrimental effect of sin on his relationship with Sarai, as well as the change of relationship with Lot, that would result in division between the two of them.

These changes ultimately manifested themselves in the fourth stumbling block as fighting broke out between the herdsmen of Lot and the herdsmen of Abram. Family dissension is the result of one bad decision followed by another, when no one is in charge. When there is no true authority governing your life, you will find yourself in a free-for-all where each person is vying for a piece of the pie.

This brings us to the final stumbling block of frustration when Abram realized that something had to change. "Where do I go from here?" he asked himself. The answer was not that complicated. The only way to overcome bad decisions is with good ones, and Abram made three great decisions that end up putting him back on his feet. First, he chose to leave Egypt. Though Egypt had already affected Lot thus affecting Abram's family, and though the fullness of the damage would not be revealed until years to come, staying there would only worsen the problem, affecting generations to come. So Abram headed north out of bondage.

His next decision was almost equal in its impact: he decided to leave Lot behind, for now he had found himself again camping between Bethel and Hai. Abram knew full well in his heart now that Lot would never follow him to his final destination with God. He also knew that a decision to stay with Lot would only result in the forfeiting of his own destiny. It was time for him to make his final decision to go back to Bethel, back to that place where he had last experienced God's presence, back to the place where he last heard His voice. Abram was ready now for God to intervene. Bruised and tattered, he looked into the face of a loving Father who picked him up, dusted off the dust of Egypt and kissed away the pain of his lost relationship with Lot.

God begins the process all over again, but now everything appears to have changed for Abram. Though still in a healing mode, he seems wiser than he did the first time and as in most cases, his stumbling blocks would serve as stepping stones toward the future, enabling him to walk on a higher plain than he had originally thought. Though the scars of his failure would never be permanently removed, over the course of time, they would eventually become to Abram a trophy of God's grace and mercy, enabling those who would follow his example to trust God with their life and destiny. Would this be his last failure? Would he find himself on his face again? These questions for now seem too difficult to consider. Now is the time to rest, if but for a moment, in the arms of the Father.

Chapter Three

Abram the Warrior

Genesis 14:14- "And when Abram heard that his brother was taken captive, he armed his trained servants, born in his own house, three hundred and eighteen, and pursued them unto Dan."

Abram found himself back on the plains of Mamre, back in proper relationship with God, back with his family, with the distraction of Lot behind him and the mistake of Egypt forgiven. Now he breathed a sigh of relief. He has made it back to ground zero, back to where he started, realizing now that it is equally possible to lose ground as well as gain it.

I can relate (as we all can) to what Abram is feeling right now, since the walk of faith seems like it's one step forward and two steps back, where we spend a lot more time on our face than on our feet. I know in my own life, I struggled with what I call the wandering years. I experienced God in a dramatic way when I was only nine years old. Though it was in many ways the most difficult time in my own history, it was also the most pivotal. It seems to work like that more often than not. My mother had experienced a nervous breakdown, shortly after my mentally challenged sister had grown severely worse, requiring us to place her in a mental facility in Danville, KY. The screams of my sister's epileptic seizures were replaced with the screams of my mother as she experienced nightmares brought on by the panic connected to the whole situation. I, on the other hand, was trying to cope with the loss of my sister and the struggles of my mother at the same time. I wondered what normal would be like from here on.

After a long absence from church due to my mother's health, we were able to return and God chose to manifest His power in an awesome display. It would forever be fixed in my memory as He literally raised a man from his wheelchair, healed my sister of a goiter which vanished before my eyes, and touched my mother. I was assured instantly that He was aware of my need and that He was more than enough for the challenges that life could bring. Yet like Abram, I wandered off on my own shortly thereafter. The farther I wandered, the more lost I became until I found myself seven or eight years later totally lost and in need of a Savior to redeem and restore my life.

For I discovered, like Abram, that sin will take you farther than you want to go, keep you longer than you want to stay, and cost you more than you're willing to pay. It had been seven years since Abram had struck out on his own. His own family dynamics had changed dramatically in the process, with each member carrying his own particular scars from the failed journey. Abram must have also wondered what normal would look like from here on, since normal is a relative term always changing.

Still carrying the scars of yesteryear, he started all over again with peace within but totally unaware of the war that is brewing on the horizon. The surrounding nations were planning an attack on Sodom. The news finally reached Abram that Lot had been taken as a prisoner of war. Abram would now be faced with a decision: to go to war for Lot or to play it safe in Bethel. This choice is one we live out every day in the life of the church. Of course, it's easy to say that Lot had made his choice; let him suffer the consequences. But the question we must honestly consider is this: how can we sit here inside the safety of the church while our brothers and sisters experience the cruelty of their captors?

Like Abram, we must learn the valuable lesson that the price of restoration, though it is free, requires everything of us, in order to become the restorer of the fallen. Galatians 6:1 puts it this way, "Brethren, if a man be overtaken in a fault, ye which are spiritual, restore such an one in the spirit of meekness; considering thyself, lest thou also be tempted." Abram would have to give up safety for a sword and replace peace with a pursuit, one that would take him all the way to Dan, the most extreme border of Israel. Sometime or another we will be faced with a decision to lay it all on the line for the salvation of another. It is the reasonable price for those that have been restored. But how do we do it, especially when we have lived our lives more as a victim than a victor and since we feel less than trained as a soldier of war? The first step in restoring is to remember the pain of our own imprisonment. Again in Galatians 6:1, we read, ".....restore such an one in the spirit of meekness; considering thyself...." If we keep forever in the forefront of our mind, our own past failures, our weaknesses, our propensity toward sin and even our own need of restoration in one area or another, it will keep us away from the snares of judgmentalism or self-righteousness that await all of us who dare to restore another from the pit.

Secondly, we must be willing to deal honestly with the weaknesses in our own lives. For the danger is always present for us to fall into the same trap from which we seek to pull our brother. We must be ever aware that scripture warns us to beware when ye think you stand, lest you fall. Proceed with caution with your arms fully open and your heart and mind guarded against the attack of the enemy.

Thirdly, we must be willing to carry the burden of the fallen for a little while. Galatians 6:2 declares, "Bear ye one another's burdens, and so fulfill the law of Christ." As Jesus bore our sin and shame publicly on a cross for all to see, we too must be willing to bear the burden of our fallen comrades, fully aware of the fact that sin brings with it shame, and there is disgrace in failure. It is the ugly truth that cannot be disguised by our feeble attempts to cover ourselves. We look as ridiculous as Adam and Eve in their tailored fig leaves, yet naked before the all-seeing eyes of our Father.

Fourthly, we must remain humble and refuse to engage in the comparison game. The Bible teaches us in 2 Corinthians 10:12, "For we dare not make ourselves of the number, or compare ourselves with some that commend themselves: but they measuring themselves by themselves, and comparing themselves among themselves, are not wise." The answer to this dilemma is to have a true sense of value, knowing your weaknesses as well as your strengths. This war zone is not the place for false humility. We must heed the words of Galatians 6:3: "For if a man think himself to be something, when he is nothing, he deceiveth himself."

Fifthly, we must stay committed through the ups and downs that are sure to follow. Or as Galatians 6:4 puts it, "But let every man prove his own work, and then shall he have rejoicing in himself alone, and not in another." We must be wise enough to know that a war is made up of many battles, those we will lose as well as the many we will win. But our confidence must be in the fact that we are ourselves the living proof that our God is a restorer of the fallen. Our rejoicing must be in His ability rather than in visible progress; for the restoration process will have its ups and downs. We must not give up the battle until we have secured the victory.

And last but not least; we must remember the sixth and final step in the restorative process found in Galatians 6:5: "For every man shall bear his own burden." We can never overlook that fact of personal responsibility. Our objective as a restorer is to bring that person back to the place of a personal decision. Where he goes from there depends on the choices that he makes. The final outcome is not your responsibility.

This is what Abram was about to discover as he set off to restore Lot, who would not make it all the way back to Bethel, the house of God. Lot would choose to return to Sodom. As we see in Genesis 14:16-17, "¹⁶And he brought back all the goods, and also brought again his brother Lot, and his goods, and the women also, and the people. ¹⁷And the king of Sodom went out to meet him after his return from the slaughter of Chedorlaomer, and of the kings that were with him, at the valley of Shaveh, which is the king's dale." Abram had to leave Lot in the valley of decision, while he makes his way back up the mountain toward Bethel. No doubt, he was disappointed with the situation, but nevertheless had the assurance that he had done all that was expected of him as a restorer of his brother.

This is all any of us can ever hope for when we venture out to become the restorers of the fallen. We will win some and lose some. Most of the time, however, it will be too complex to know right away. Lot's restoration was completed when rescued by God before destruction hits the city of Sodom. But had not Abram done his job and brought Lot back to Sodom, it would have ultimately hindered his final restoration. In God's great plan of redemption, we all have a role to play that vitally connects us one to another, forming the picture of God's grace for the world to view.

It is also crucial as restorers that we never forget the weapons that God has made available to us as a part of our arsenal. Without them, our chances of success are nil and our personal danger increases in the process.

There happens to be five of them which I consider intriguing since five is the number of grace.

The first is the Word of God. No trained soldier would ever consider going to battle without his sword, and truly the Word of God serves as our protection against the enemy as well as our weapon to counteract his ploys.

Second is the power of the Holy Spirit. He works hand in hand with the Word of God to ensure the victory, not only in the lives we seek to restore but in our lives as well as we wage battle. It's "...not by might, nor by power, but by my spirit, saith the Lord of hosts" that every lasting victory is won. (Zechariah 4:6)

Third is the name of Jesus. What a wonderful blessing that Jesus Himself has given us the authority as believers to use His name! His name is above every name and at the mention of His name, everything must bow in submission. Even at the mention of His name demons tremble, hell is shaken, and all heaven stands at attention.

Next is the fourth weapon, His blood. This serves as a constant reminder to the devil of the victory that Jesus purchased on the cross. Through the blood, we enforce our right as believers to walk in the fullness of our liberty, reversing the curse and annihilating the hold of the enemy upon our lives.

And the last weapon is the truth. Jesus Himself said in John 8:32, "And ye shall know the truth, and the truth shall make you free." We are the carriers of that truth which has the ability to break the chains of bondage, setting the captives free and establishing a foundation upon which they can construct a brand new life. "⁴For the weapons of our warfare are not carnal, but mighty through God to the pulling down of strongholds; ⁵Casting down imaginations, and every high thing that exalteth itself against the knowledge of God, and bringing into captivity every thought to the obedience of Christ;" (2 Corinthians 10:4-5) With our weapon in hand and God's purpose at heart, God has fully prepared us, like Abram, to restore the fallen back to the place of decision.

Abram headed home, exhausted but gratified in knowing that Lot was home again with his family; he could rest a little easier and enjoy his own restoration more fully now knowing that not only had he freely received, but he had given as well, becoming a conduit of God's grace to the world. After all, isn't that what restoration is all about. Well done, Abram! Take your rest and enjoy your spoils.

Chapter Four

Abram the Worshipper

*Genesis 14:20-"And blessed be the most high God, which
hath delivered thine enemies into thy hand. And he gave
him tithes of all."*

Sweaty, exhausted and somewhat frustrated, Abram returned from battle,
having recovered Lot from the hands of his captors. Yet no doubt he was
disappointed in the fact that Lot was choosing to return to Sodom, the
very place from which he was captured in the first place. These types of
decisions cause all of us as restorers to scratch our heads and wonder if
anything has changed or if people ever learn even a single lesson from the
pain they encounter at the hand of their adversary. One thing is clear,
however. If there is no change in the nature of a person, we should not
expect there to be a change in their actions. As the old story goes, you can
give a pig a bath, paint its hoofs with nail polish, put a ribbon around
his neck and squirt him with perfume. But when you let him go, he will
head right back for the mud hole. Why? Simply put, he is still a pig by
nature and you can never hope to change his actions until he experiences
a change in that nature. This is where we must experience the intervention
of God. Only He can change the nature of man, resulting in the change of
his actions as well as his destiny. Abram has learned a valuable lesson: he
can get Lot out of prison but only God Himself can set him free.

In this moment of weakness and disappointment, Abram encountered
God afresh and anew through the High Priest and King Melchizedek. As
we know, throughout the Old Testament, the king, the priest, and the
prophet were three distinct roles of Kingdom authority. To cross these

boundaries was unlawful, resulting in the judgment of God. We see examples of this judgment in the lives of Saul, Uzziah and others as they took lightly the order of God. Yet this man, Melchizedek, was the king of righteousness, the king of peace, and the priest of the most High according Hebrews 7:1-2. Verse 3 goes on to describe him, "Without father, without mother, without descent, having neither beginning of days, nor end of life; but made like unto the Son of God; abideth a priest continually." This description has led many theologians to conclude that Melchizedek was in actuality a pre-incarnate appearance of Jesus Christ Himself. But nonetheless we know for certain that Abram experienced God, as is often the case in a moment of weakness and despair, and he will learn a valuable lesson that all of us must learn at one time or another. Worship has nothing to do with our circumstances, for worship centers around His worth and His worth is unchanging. Therefore we must learn the power of worship in the bad times as well as the good. In fact, Abram's ability to worship at this moment would ultimately set the stage for Lot's future deliverance.

Worship is in fact a learned behavior; though all of us, I believe, are born with what I refer to as the God vacuum, desiring to know our Creator in an intimate way. Yet cultures have revealed over time that the pursuit of this relationship can take on a variety of acts and rituals, shaped by our history, traditions, education, environment, and a host of other factors that shape our expressions of worship.

Yet Abram, in this brief encounter, will teach us seven principles of true and authentic worship. This type of worship will in turn enhance our relationship with God, realigning our attitude and establishing our feet like hind's feet as we walk out the victory provided by the cross. For these are principles of worship that go far beyond the act of worship itself; these are foundation stones on which our lives can be constructed that will enable us to withstand the winds of adversity that are sure to blow as we walk out the life of faith.

The first lesson taught to us by the father of the faithful is that worship is recognition of the presence and intervention of God in our everyday lives. Abram was unwilling to assume the credit for his victory or to give the credit to the 318 that joined him for the battle. He fully understood that if the battle is the Lord's, then so also is the victory. God has not created us to operate as free agents but He is a God of interaction, choosing to involve Himself in the internal affairs of His creation from the lowly task of feeding the sparrows to the ultimate task of redeeming humanity. God is the God of bloody, dirty hands, soiled by the affairs of our everyday lives, and He is worthy of our recognition and praise.

Secondly, Abram is teaching us that worship is a time of intimate communion. It is not by chance that Melchizedek arrives with bread and wine, symbolizing the broken body and the shed blood of the new covenant received at the table of the Lord. Worship was never intended to be a drive-by event served through a fast-food window on the road of life. Rather, it is a time to rest for a while at the table of the Lord, a time to reflect on the price that was paid for your freedom. It is a time to acknowledge the covenant between you and your Father through the finished work of Christ that opened the door for your entry into the family of God, assuring you of your seat at the table of the Lord. These elements serve as a constant reminder of our position and the sweet communion that awaits us all who have a relationship with God and who recognize the table in our Father's house is always spread with His mercy and grace.

Thirdly, Abram teaches us that worship positions us in our proper place of submission, while in turn, recognizing the greatness of our God. The act of bowing in worship results in the magnification of the object of our worship. Though in reality, we can do nothing to magnify God since He is already more grand than we are able to grasp in our wildest dreams or imagination. Yet bowing in worship is a personal recognition of His greatness that exists from eternity past to eternity future. Worship doesn't change God but reveals the change that has occurred in us concerning our perception of Him.

Fourthly, worship indicates value that receives our response. One of the definitions of the word "worship" is to "lick the hand." It is a picture of a grateful dog that fully understands the role his master has played in his life by rescuing him from the harsh world outside, inviting him to become a part of the family, meeting all of his medical needs, and providing his every meal. It is a relationship by which he is protected from those that would destroy him if they were given access. He would look up at his master with no real way to repay him for his bountiful blessing. The act of merely licking the hand of his master would be his humble way to say "thanks." This is truly what worship is: a feeble attempt to repay God for all He has done as we recognize Him as the Master and ourselves as His servants. Abram does this by giving a tenth of all that he has to Melchizedek. From a grateful heart, he is recognizing that, without God, there would be no victory, no spoils of battle, and no tithe to give. The tenth is merely a lick toward the hand of God.

Fifthly, worship proves our allegiance to the Kingdom of God. I love Abram's response to the king of Sodom found in Genesis 14:22-23, "²²And Abram said to the king of Sodom, I have lift up mine hand unto the LORD, the most high God, the possessor of heaven and earth, ²³That I will not take from a thread even to a shoe latchet, and that I will not take any thing that is thine, lest thou shouldest say, I have made Abram rich:" There is no doubt here, friend, whose side he is on. And because his allegiance to God is firmly set, the ransoms of the world offered no temptation whatsoever to Abram. Oh, that God would bring all of us to that place where the amenities this world has to offer would fail in comparison to the wealth we have discovered from the place of a worshipper with uplifted hands, like our example, Abram.

Sixthly, worship provokes the blessing of God upon our lives. Genesis 14:19 declares, "And he blessed him, and said, Blessed be Abram of the most high God, possessor of heaven and earth:" How intriguing that this is the same statement ascribed back to God through the mouth of Abram in verse 22. But in this verse, it is being used to show that the blessing of Abram was that he himself belongs to God and that divine ownership in him made Abram the owner and overseer of all that God possesses in both heaven and earth. How true it is that we are heirs of God and joint heirs with Christ! And if we are willing to suffer with Him, we will be glorified to rule and reign with Him both now and throughout eternity. That is the blessing that true and authentic worship produces.

Finally, Abram teaches that true worship produces deliverance and actuates victory in our lives. Notice verse 20: "And blessed be the most high God, which hath delivered thine enemies into thy hand. And he gave him tithes of all." We must never forget that our deliverance, as well as the victories that we experience in the flesh, were first procured through the Spirit. In other words, we live out His victory that won the battle over the forces of darkness. As 2 Corinthians 2:14 states, "Now thanks be unto God, which always causeth us to triumph in Christ, and maketh manifest the savour of his knowledge by us in every place." A triumph in early days was nothing more than a victory parade, much like those that were held in America at the end of World War II. Except in a triumph, the prisoners of war were placed in the front of the parade as they marched toward the city square. At the beginning of the parade, incense would be lit, filling the city with the smell of victory while serving as a constant reminder to those prisoners of war that they were soon to die in the courtyard of authority. My what a picture of worship as with every breath, we fill the air with the sweet smelling savour of victory, exalting God as the ultimate champion of the universe while simultaneously reminding the devil of his impending doom! To us who are saved, it is the smell of victory but to those who are perishing, it is the smell of death. Thus our victory and deliverance has as much to do with our worship as it does our sword.

Abram's brief encounter with Melchizedek would forever lay the foundation for all worshippers to build upon for generations to come; yet at the same time it would serve as a guidepost, enabling him to realign himself with the purpose of God. This would serve to steady his feet for the journey ahead. Still the journey is not over yet. This is merely one step in the long walk of faith. There will be more battles to fight and more lessons to learn before Abram will arrive at the destiny God has planned for his life. But for now, he is back on his feet and focused on the One that is more than enough for the journey.

So with a quick embrace, Abram leaves Lot in the hands of God in Sodom and begins to make his way back to Bethel, completely unaware that there is company awaiting him back home. There a mystery guest awaits him who will ultimately unlock the secret steps to the walk of faith, not only for Abram and his family but for all of us that seek to follow in his footsteps. So hurry up, Abram! We're all waiting on you to arrive.

Chapter Five

Abram's Walk of Faith

Genesis 15:6-"And Abram believed the Lord, and the Lord
counted him righteous because of his faith." NLT

As the hot desert winds blew hard across the plains of Mamre, suddenly the flap on Abram's tent blew open with a snap, revealing a torch in the distance. Someone was coming straight for Abram's camp, but who could it be? He had left Lot in Sodom; no one else even knew where Abram was camping. As he stood there wondering in his heart, this mystery guest drew closer and closer till their eyes met in the flickering light of the torch. Abram was speechless as he looked into the eyes of this man or was he a man at all? Or was he an angel? All these questions flooded his mind for his face looked faintly familiar. Was this Melchizedek? Though the guest resembled him, something was different this time. For this face was filled with love, a love like Abram had never known. Abram bowed at the waist, inviting him to come in but to his surprise, the guest invited him to come outside instead.

"Could this be a dream?" he must have wondered. For he was no longer on the plains of Mamre, but he found himself in Bethlehem looking down on a little stable where a young mother sat quietly by a manger, holding a newborn son, surrounded by shepherds and wise men and angels, all worshipping in unison and praising God for His wonderful gift of love. Could it be the promised seed that God had told him would come? The scene was much too holy for Abram to break the silence with a question now. So he looked on as the next scene seemed to unfold in panoramic glory. Before his eyes, a young lad appeared, growing in favor with God and man. "Surely He must be the one," he thought. But when will He bring deliverance as God had promised? He seemed like a normal child just playing in the streets of Nazareth.

Then all at once, his ears were filled with the voice of one crying in the wilderness, "Prepare ye the way of the Lord." Who could this curious fellow be, dressed in a leather girdle and camel hair, baptizing and warning people of the judgment to come as they gathered on the banks of the Jordan River? John held up his hands to silence the crowd as he pointed to one coming as he said, "Behold the Lamb of God that takes away the sins of the world." Abram watched intently as John baptized this same man as the skies opened. A dove descended and lit upon Him, as a thunderous voice spoke from Heaven saying, "This is my beloved Son in whom I am well pleased."

Abram continued to watch from the balcony of time as the Son of God healed the sick, raised the dead, opened blinded eyes, and preached the Gospel to the poor, the brokenhearted, and downtrodden. Surely this was more than a shepherd's mind could contain. What could possibly happen next? To Abram's surprise, he watched as an angry mob shouted "Crucify." The same crowd that had days before shouted, "Hosanna" had turned violently against the one that they had previously desired to make their king. He watched as He was arrested, falsely accused, beaten, and then crucified. "Is that it? Is this all?" he must have thought as the picture went dark and the earth stood in silence. Abram was much too afraid now to speak and not even sure of what he would say if given the chance. So he waited quietly with all humanity for what seemed like an eternity. Then beneath his feet, the earth began to shake and a light brighter than the noonday sun struck the earth like an anvil. The rocks quaked and the tomb that held the body of this man lit up as a giant stone rolled away. Choirs of angels filled the earth with praise, for death could not hold Him. "He's alive---He's alive," they shouted, "And He lives forevermore."

Watching from a distance, it was all he could do to hold his peace as his heart was filled with hope of what would someday come. "What would happen now?" is the question that filled his mind as over the next several days he watched the Son of God interact with His disciples. Then one day in particular, on a hill filled with olive trees, he listened as He spoke to them, encouraging them to go into all the world and preach the Gospel to every nation, as gravity lost its hold on Him. Abram watched along with the disciples as He ascended into the heavens and took his seat at the right hand of the throne of God. As he pondered all these things in his heart, he suddenly could feel once again the desert sand around his feet as he stood in the doorway of his tent again, still gazing into the eyes of this same man. But now the mystery was gone for he knew this was Jesus, the Son of the living God, the Word of God made flesh. The mystery had now been replaced by revelation, a revelation of faith, which would serve as the foundation upon which every step of faith would come to rest.

Standing there in darkness, with only a torch to serve as light, the hand of Jesus directed his eyes upward to the sky above. "Do you see the stars, Abram, My friend?" the question rang out in the darkness. "Can you number them or call them by name?" As he searched for an answer, the voice of Jesus spoke out again, saying, "So shall your seed be, without number." Then came the question that would seal the deal in Abram's life and future, "Do you believe that I am able to perform all the things that I have shown unto you?" Now was time for his response.

This revelation of faith would be followed by a second step in the walk of faith that all of us must take: that desire to become a friend of God. It is the confession of faith as Genesis 15:6 and Galatians 3:6-7 declare that Abram believed and confessed this same Jesus as Lord. The key is found in the Hebrew word for *believe*. It translates *Ah-mahn* or as we would pronounce it, *Amen* or "so be it unto me." It is not just an inward agreement with truth but an inward agreement coupled with an outward verbal expression incorporating both heart and mouth. Meeting the criteria and conditions for salvation is found in Romans 10:9-10, "⁹That if thou shalt confess with thy mouth the Lord Jesus, and shalt believe in thine heart that God hath raised Him from the dead, thou shalt be saved. ¹⁰For with the heart man believeth unto righteousness; and with the mouth confession is made unto salvation."

Abram had witnessed firsthand the finished work of Jesus, though in reality it wouldn't take place for some 2,161 years. Yet Jesus Himself signed on as Abram's witness that this was a true and authentic vision from God. In John 8:56, He declared before all Israel, "Your father Abraham rejoiced to see my day: and he saw it, and was glad." Now we who desire to walk the walk of faith look backward 2000 years at the finished work of Jesus and by faith, accept it as the basis of the new covenant. We realize that without faith, it is impossible to please Him, for he that cometh to God must believe that He is, and that He is the rewarder of those that diligently seek Him.

What Abram discovered next is not only a crucial step for him but for all of us that choose to walk out the covenant of faith. It is found in the fact that the walk of faith is much more than just a revelation of faith followed by a confession, but that this confession must be followed by a commitment containing all that we are and all that we possess. When he asked Jesus for evidence of this invisible covenant, the Lord's response must have taken Abram by surprise. He required Abram to sacrifice a three-year-old heifer, a three-year-old ram, a three-year-old goat, a turtledove, and a young pigeon. There is a tremendous lesson to be learned here for all of us. A simple confession without a commitment is as fruitless as a wedding without a marriage to follow: vain words spoken without true intent.

What would follow this commitment? Abram was about to discover the statement all of us have used: We are in a fight of faith. For scripture tells us in Genesis 15:11, "Then birds of prey came down on the carcasses, but Abram drove them away." (NIV) He learned that every commitment will be challenged, every sacrifice tested, and we must be willing to stand guard against the attack of the enemy and defend our sacrifice. Only the commitments we keep can God receive and reward. After all, there is no reward for feeding buzzards with intended sacrifices. That only leads to victimization, not victory. The fight of faith must be won through persistence, and reward comes only to those who endure. So we can see plainly the progression as Abram walks out the steps of faith, making his way from the revelation of faith to the confession of faith, to the commitment of faith, to the fight of faith. But what came next must certainly have looked inviting to Abram as God invited him to rest.

He took his much needed nap, but God was not yet finished. God did not desire Abram's interference in this part of the covenant. Since a covenant is only as strong as its weakest link, God chose in His wisdom to make a covenant with Himself that would never be broken. A burning lamp representing His living word and a smoking furnace representing the Holy Spirit passed between the sacrifice in a figure eight pattern (the number signifies a new beginning). This served as a constant reminder of new life offered through the unbreakable covenant between the Father and the Son, and witnessed by the Holy Spirit Himself. This all occurred while Abram rested for a moment from the fight of faith. He awoke to a brand new covenant filled with blessing and benefits.

The sixth step revealed the covenant blessings that drew out in detail the boundaries of the royal grant that would be promised to the descendant of Abram. They stretched from the rivers of Egypt to the great river Euphrates, encompassing the land of the Kenites, the Kenizzites, the Kadmonites, the Hittites, the Perizzites, the Rephaites, the Amorites, the Canaanites, the Girgashites, and the Jebusites. Though all these people still presently lived in the land, this land now belonged to Abram and to Israel by the declaration of God Himself. They must be willing to dispossess it from the enemy and possess it for Kingdom purposes. This became known as what I refer to as the Great Commission of the Old Testament: to secure the land, the royal grant where Christ will reign during his millennial reign upon the earth. The New Testament Great Commission centers on securing the inhabitants of the land from every kindred, tribe, and tongue.

The seventh and final step in the walk of faith brings us full circle back to verse 1 of Genesis 15 as we discover, along with Abram, the benefits of this new covenant. Now let me explain that benefits are different from blessings. For where blessings appear to be automatic, benefits on the other hand must be appropriated. We will find hidden in this one verse six benefits neatly packaged in six words used for the first time in scripture, each one revealing what Adam lost due to sin. Abram, and all of us who walk by faith, have gained access to them again by putting our faith in the finished work of Christ. These six words hold the six secret benefits of the walk of faith.

Word

Genesis 15:1 is the first time we find "word" listed in the Bible. As we all know, words are necessary in order for communication to take place. When Adam was created and placed in the Garden of Eden, part of the benefit package of Adam's covenant with God was that he and God talked together while strolling through the garden in the cool of the day. But when Adam sinned against God he was driven from the garden; and due to Adam's sin, communication with God was severed. But when we, by faith, enter into covenant with God through faith in Jesus Christ, communication is reestablished with God through our covenant benefit of prayer. It is important that we appropriate this benefit. We need to heed the invitation of Hebrews 4:16: "Let us therefore come boldly unto the throne of grace, that we may obtain mercy, and find grace to help in time of need."

Vision

Appearing in Genesis 15:1, this is also the first time the word "vision" is used in the Bible. Vision naturally has to do with our ability to see things clearly as they truly are. When God created Adam, he was created with the ability to see fully in the realm of the Spirit. But when he sinned, something happened to his eyesight. The eyes of the flesh were opened and he saw that he was naked. Also he lost the ability to peek into the realms of the Spirit. When we, by faith, covenant with God like Abram did, once again God opens the eyes of our spirit to receive the things that are hidden to the natural eye. As 1 Corinthians 2:9-10 declares, "But as it is written, Eye hath not seen, nor ear heard, neither have entered into the heart of man, the things which God hath prepared for them that love him. But God hath revealed them unto us by his Spirit: for the Spirit searcheth all things, yea, the deep things of God."

Revelation, illumination, and even the ability to see anything from God's perspective is just another benefit of our faith covenant.

Fear Not

Again, Genesis 15:1 is the first time in scripture when we read the words "fear not". When Adam and Eve were created and placed in the garden, there was no need to fear, for love surrounded them as they walked out the plan of God in perfect harmony with Him. But when Adam sinned, fear was birthed, and Adam hid himself from the presence of

God. When by faith we once again covenant with God, fear is banished and replaced by love. As 1 John 4:18 declares, "There is no fear in love; but perfect love casteth out fear: because fear hath torment. He that feareth is not made perfect in love." Three hundred sixty-five times the Bible commands us to fear not. But the choice is still ours. Either we can appropriate the benefit of our love relationship with God through Jesus Christ, allowing Him to make us perfect in love, or fear will dominate our life.

I Am

"I Am" is used for the first time in Scripture in Genesis 15:1. God would speak them later to Moses, assuring him that whatever he needed God to be, he could trust that He was the great I Am. I Am represents God's provisional name for our lives. Adam and Eve lived in a perfect environment with all the provisions they would ever need furnished by the hand of God Himself. But when they sinned, they were banished from the garden and were required to gain their own provision through effort and sweat.

When by faith we enter into a faith covenant with God as Abram did, the provision of God is established in our lives as a benefit of that covenant relationship. As children of God, we can firmly hold to the promise, "But my God shall supply all your need according to his riches in glory by Christ Jesus." (Philippians 4:19) We will also be able to echo David's words, "I have been young, and now am old; yet have I not seen the righteous forsaken, nor his seed begging bread" (Psalm 37:25.)

Once again, let me remind you that these are benefits of a faith covenant that must be appropriated as we obediently follow the scriptures given to us concerning tithing and giving. Benefits are not automatic; we must meet the criteria.

Shield

The word "shield" is also introduced in Genesis 15:1. Shield represents our covering, our protection. Before sin, Adam and Eve were naked and unashamed because they were covered by the grace and love of God, protected from harm by God Himself. But when they sinned, God's hand was removed and instantly they felt change occur—they were naked, exposed, and in danger. Just as all humanity tries to cover its sinful nakedness, Adam and Eve sought to cover themselves with leaves. But their attempt failed, just as all attempts after them have failed.

But through faith in Christ, we enter into the faith covenant with God where we are once again covered with His love and His mercy and protected by His power. As we appropriate this benefit by heeding the words of Ephesians 6:16: "Above all, taking the shield of faith, wherewith ye shall be able to quench all the fiery darts of the wicked. "

Reward

"Reward" is the final first word of Genesis 15:1. When Adam and Eve were created and placed in the garden, it was a paradise, a perfect environment, where they not only enjoyed their relationship with one another, but their relationship with God as well. When sin entered the picture, everything changed. They lost the reward of paradise and in its place gained the penalty of death.

When by faith we accept the finished work of Jesus Christ on the cross, the opposite occurs—we lose the penalty of death in our lives and gain the reward of eternal paradise with Him. We hold to the promise, "[1]Let not your heart be troubled: ye believe in God, believe also in me. [2]In my Father's house are many mansions: if it were not so, I would have told you I go to prepare a place for you. [3]And if I go and prepare a place for you, I will come again, and receive you unto myself; that where I am, there ye may be also." (John 14:1-3)

As Abram stood there pondering all the richness of this newfound covenant with God and all the blessings and benefits it entailed, suddenly a gust of wind embraced his face with a kiss of reality as he slowly opened his eyes to discover that he was alone again, standing under the stars, imagining each one to be his very own child. It all seemed a little overwhelming-Abram still looked exactly the same but God, on the other hand, looked totally different. He realized now that God was able to do more than he had ever imagined and with the glimpse of the future still fresh in his mind, he was now ready to walk it out. Much too excited to go back inside the tent, he decided to linger for awhile and dream. Tomorrow will be a new day filled with its own challenges but for now, it is time to bask in God's presence and reflect on His goodness.

Chapter Six

Abram's Half Time

Isaiah 40:30- "But they that wait upon the LORD shall renew their strength; they shall mount up with wings as eagles; they shall run, and not be weary; and they shall walk, and not faint."

As days turned into weeks, weeks into months and months into years, Abram found himself struggling with his faith. What seemed hard to believe over a decade ago grew more impossible with every passing day. The vision that had revolutionized his life seemed little more than a dream now, a dream filled with questions of how and when. God had promised him a child. In fact, He had promised a nation would come from his loins. But every wrinkle that creased his face and every painful joint stood in defiance to the promise of God as he found himself entering the halfway zone. I call it halftime: halfway between the promise and the answer, between vision and reality, between barrenness and fruitfulness. Abram would be the first to experience halftime but certainly not the last. Moses, Nehemiah, and a host of others would witness this phenomenon and teach us how to navigate these troubled waters. But Abram would have to go it alone. He would soon discover that the decisions you make in halftime are critical ones. Not only can they affect your life, but also the lives of generations to come.

Abram's first bad decision was to allow the voice of human reasoning to face off against the word of the Lord. When we allow our own human reasoning to get involved in the process, we open the door to the enemy of faith. Romans 8:6-8 declares: "⁶For to be carnally minded is death; but to be spiritually minded is life and peace. ⁷Because the carnal mind is enmity against God: for it is not subject to the law of God, neither indeed can be. [8]So then they that are in the flesh cannot please God." All of us must remember Isaiah 55:8-9 as God declares, "[8]For my thoughts are not your thoughts, neither are your ways my ways, saith the Lord. [9]For as the heavens are higher than the earth, so are my ways higher than your ways, and my thoughts than your thoughts." Abram was now the rope in a tug of war between his flesh and his spirit. As often the case, our own human reasoning leads to the next step: devise a human plan. Now that we have taken the problem into our own hands, we feel we must deliver ourselves from the dilemma we have created in our minds. God had a plan but now Abram had a plan; which plan would win out? And even a bigger question emerges: Who is in charge?

Abram's second step on the slippery slope was to forfeit his leadership role as the head of his household; decisions were now being made by popular opinion. Everyone was discussing the problem now and Sarai's insecurity would be the driving force in the newfound plan of how this promised child would be born. Abram would discover yet another truth: "When everyone's in charge, no one's in charge!" Leadership is a vacuum. Bad leadership arises when real leaders refuse to lead or take a stand. God had called Abram to lead his family through halftime. But now he was being led into a plan devised by human reasoning that could only produce human results as he hearkened to the voice of Sarai.

The third lesson Abram would discover in this halftime moment is one we must always remember: what is born of the flesh must be sustained by the flesh. Everything seemed fine at first as the plan was executed without a hitch, but soon the faulty plan would fall apart at the seams and the blame game would begin. Ironically, Sarai was the first to launch the attack on Abram as she declared, "My wrong be upon thee." (Genesis 16:5) The reins of leadership were placed again in his hands; now he must devise a plan of recovery from the human plan. But innocent lives were involved in the mess, feelings were hurt, division was imminent, and things would never be the same.

There are two more lessons to learn before halftime ends, but they just might be the most important. Abram would soon discover the difference between blessing and covenant. Though God would redeem the situation and in fact, He would promise to bless Ishmael and his seed, he would not be the son of covenant promise. Since God would not allow any flesh to glory in His presence, He had put Abram in a deep sleep to restrain him from involvement and made a covenant with Himself. God knew well that if man was involved in the covenant, man would also be the weak link in the chain and the covenant would eventually fall victim to man's weakness. Abram suddenly remembered that he was nothing more than a recipient of the covenant between God the Father and God the Son. And so are we.

There's only one lesson left to learn but it is significant. It is simple yet profound. It sounds easy but it goes against all we think or feel. We must wait on God. Abram had another decade or more before God would fulfill the promise to him, but with halftime now behind him and Ishmael, along with the family division before his eyes, he was willing to submit himself for the duration of time. No matter how long it would take, he would wait patiently on God to perform His word.

As every leader learns, waiting on God is a process that changes us from the inside out. The benefits of waiting are far beyond our imagination while the act of waiting itself grinds against our intellect, emotions and will. The pain is almost unbearable, but the benefits outweigh the pain. Isaiah 40:31 declares, "But they that wait upon the LORD shall renew their strength; they shall mount up with wings as eagles; they shall run, and not be weary; and they shall walk, and not faint."

James 1:2-5 says, "²My brethren, count it all joy when ye fall into divers temptations; ³Knowing this, that the trying of your faith worketh patience. ⁴But let patience have her perfect work, that ye may be perfect and entire, wanting nothing. ⁵If any of you lack wisdom, let him ask of God, that giveth to all men liberally, and upbraideth not; and it shall be given him." Waiting is the process God chooses to bring us to a place of completion and wholeness. Waiting produces in the Christian life what nothing else can. Waiting empties our soul of self-dependency; as we wait upon the Lord, we come to a place where we are no longer offering God our opinions, but rather we become willing to obey Him at all cost.

Secondly, waiting weakens the flesh and brings us to a place of subjection and submission. At the same time, waiting strengthens our spirit man, bringing us to a place of spiritual authority. Before salvation, our soul and our spirit were enslaved by our flesh. We operated by our five senses, with our soul and spirit following along like a well-trained puppy. Once our spirit became born again, we found ourselves in a struggle-to renew our mind and to restrain our flesh with all its lustful desires. How can we turn the tide and bring our soul and flesh in subjection to our spirit? The answer is by waiting on God. Waiting is the key to victory and spiritual authority!

As we can plainly see in the life of Abram, waiting on God is not a waste of time; waiting pays dividends both now and for eternity. Abram's willingness to wait on God not only ended in the fulfillment of his personal dream, but it opened the door for all of us who follow to share in the same faith covenant and its benefits and blessing. I, for one, am thankful that Abram was willing to wait. Though it was twenty-five years between the promise and the birth of Isaac, seeming long and tiresome to him as he experienced the process day by day, in the scheme of eternity, it was but a moment with benefits lasting for generations. Will the generations that follow be glad we waited on God, or will they be left to battle the works of the flesh we created?

I have discovered in my own life six benefits of waiting on God, though I must admit that waiting on God is never easy. May I offer them for your consideration?

Waiting on God strengthens our spirit man; though our flesh despises waiting, our spirit man is renewed, refreshed, and rejuvenated when we find ourselves surrounded by His presence and waiting at His feet. Psalm 46:10 declares, "Be still, and know that I am God: I will be exalted among the heathen, I will be exalted in the earth." May we quiet our spirit and listen for His heart.

Waiting challenges our intellect; it forces us to rethink every position, every decision. It causes us to hesitate and consider God's Word in light of our thoughts as well as the thoughts of those around us. We must heed the instructions of Romans 12:1-2: "[1]I beseech you therefore, brethren, by the mercies of God, that ye present your bodies a living sacrifice, holy, acceptable unto God, which is your reasonable service. [2]And be not conformed to this world: but be ye transformed by the renewing of your mind, that ye may prove what is that good, and acceptable, and perfect, will of God." As we continue to turn to the Word of the Lord, the washing of the water of the Word purifies our minds and changes the way we think, and we learn to bring every thought captive to the Word of God.

Changing our thinking results in a replacement of our desires and dreams. God indeed has a plan for every life as Jeremiah 29:11 declares: "For I know the thoughts that I think toward you, saith the LORD, thoughts of peace, and not of evil, to give you an expected end." But the struggle comes in replacing our dreams with His. In fact, it will only occur when the Word of God replaces our own thoughts. John 15:7 says, "If ye abide in me, and my words abide in you, ye shall ask what ye will, and it shall be done unto you."

New thinking and new desires bring change to our actions. It is futile to attempt to change what we are doing while ignoring who we are since our *do* comes directly from our *who*! Actions are merely the manifestations of our desires and thoughts. As we experience the inward changes, it is reflected in the way we act and treat others, bringing us to the next benefit.

Our relationships are refined. We are no longer satisfied with surface relationship but begin looking for lifelong, even eternal, relationships with those that share in our dream and visions. We start the process of turning friends to family as relationships become sacred in our lives.

Last, but not least, is the final benefit: Our dreams become reality. We are able to fully appreciate the satisfaction that comes as the destiny of God passes from faith to sight.

As Abram continued to wait on God, one thing was certain: God is back in charge and He alone is able to do what He has spoken. The God that spoke your promise is more than able to perform it. The great thing we learn from this segment in the life of Abram is this: Failure is not final; God is able to redeem us and our circumstances for His Kingdom purpose. Little did Abram realize that His next encounter with God was on the horizon and the second half of the journey would begin with the dawning of a brand new day.

Chapter Seven

Abram's Promise

*Genesis 17:2-"And I will make my covenant between me and thee,
and will multiply thee exceedingly."*

Days were filled with wonder and nights were filled with dreams, as Abram watched Ishmael grow before his very eyes. Could this be the child of promise? Would Sarai ever accept him as her own? Will the bickering ever stop? Abram had more questions than answers but one thing was certain— Abram loved Ishmael and he was determined to enjoy every moment with him; for he was the apple of his eye and the object of his affection. Yes, fatherhood was grander than Abram ever imagined.

Sarai on the other hand grew more miserable with each passing day as Hagar paraded her son before her like a trophy. She also struggled with the fact that she was no longer the focal point of Abram's life; he now lavished his love on Ishmael. And yes, Ishmael himself had become a problem to Sarai for he served as a constant reminder of her own barrenness. The mixture of joy and pain continued over the next thirteen years as Abram and Sarai struggled to bridge the gap brought about by their own lack of patience and their desire to help God to fulfill the promises given in the past.

The dawn breaks on a new day that must by now have seemed routine as any other morning. Yet soon, they would realize that on this day, the timing of God would meet the promise of God, and the will of God would soon be born. This was the day of destiny! Abram and Sarai would never be the same. In fact, everything was about to change as the Lord would appear once again, this time to fulfill all that He had promised.

As Abram went about his daily life, suddenly the Lord appeared a second time to him. The voice of the Lord shattered the stress and tension that by now seemed almost unbearable. "I am the Almighty God, walk before me and be thou perfect." Perfect and blameless hardly described the situation at hand, which by the way, was no secret to God. But this opening statement from God served as a reminder to Abram and all of us for that matter, that all we experience in our Christian life stems from our personal relationship with God-a relationship that includes our successes and failures, our joy and our pain, and our strength and our weakness. And like Abram, we all now realize that His strength is made perfect in our weakness as we put our faith not in our own strength but in His ability.

Abram now ninety-nine years old and Sarai ninety, stood in awe as God continued. Over the course of the next few minutes, the Lord would reaffirm His covenant with Abram, change their names, and seal the covenant with circumcision. Each part of this three-fold process revealed a wealth of information concerning God's heart toward Abram and his future generations.

God began by reaffirming the covenant that he had made through the vision Abram had received over twenty-four years ago, when he had been transported by the Spirit of God more than 2,000 years into the future. There he witnessed the finished work of Jesus on the cross and came to understand that all faith would come to rest on that finished work. Like a scroll unfolding, Abram began to recount the seven-fold promise that God made to him that day. It behooves all of us as believers to remember these promises since they are still in effect for all that put their faith in the finished work of Christ.

The first promise God made to Abram was to direct his path. Genesis 12:1 begins, "Now the LORD had said unto Abram, Get thee out of thy country, and from thy kindred, and from thy father's house, unto a land that I will shew thee:" God had promised to be Abram's traveling companion as well as his guide on the journey ahead. We too can rest in the promise Jesus made in Matthew 28:20, "...and, lo, I am with you alway, even unto the end of the world. Amen." You are never alone.

The second promise was found in Genesis 12:2, "And I will make of thee a great nation..." Of course we know now that Abram would become the father of Israel but, my friend, he would be much more than the father of a geo-political nation with boundaries; he would indeed become the father of a spiritual family of faith, a people without bounds, that would go beyond all limits to include every kindred, tribe, tongue and nation that would gather around the throne of God to give Him praise and glory forever. (Revelations 7:9-10)

The third promise would be just four words long but with ramifications far beyond the ability to describe, "...I will bless thee..." (Genesis 12:2) The word, *bless* in scripture reveals five different meanings, each one overwhelming in and of itself yet connected together, painting a picture of God's touch on the believer's life. Blessing means: Be well, be whole, be favored, be prosperous and be comforted by His presence. Wow! No wonder Solomon said, "The blessing of the Lord, it maketh rich, and he addeth no sorrow with it." (Proverbs 10:22)

The fourth promise, in Genesis 12:2, declares, "...and make thy name great..." God was not promising Abram his name in lights, so to speak, but rather that Abram would become great by association. As Abram would allow himself to be used as an instrument of God, in turn, as Christ was lifted up, through Him Abram too would be lifted up. The same is true for those that call themselves Christians. By covenant as well as by association, we are connected with the Great One, Christ Jesus the Savior of the world.

The fifth promise God made to Abram and His seed is also found in Genesis 12:2, "...and thou shalt be a blessing." The blessing of God cannot be contained. God's intent is for His blessing to overflow in your life into the lives of those around you. Truly blessed people affect their neighborhoods, communities, cities, states, and nations. God is indeed El Shaddai, the God that is more than enough, a God of overflowing blessing. He cannot be contained.

The sixth promise is in Genesis 12:3, "And I will bless them that bless thee, and curse him that curseth thee..." This is a promise of God's protection in the life of the believer. It places the responsibility strictly on the shoulders of God, relieving us from the need to keep records or plan our revenge on those that oppose us. God Himself has promised to cover, to protect and to defeat our enemies. Furthermore, He has promised to bless those that bless us out of the storehouse of heaven and not our storehouse.

The seventh and final promise Abram remembered is also found in Genesis 12:3, "…and in thee shall all families of the earth be blessed." This promise spoke of the seed, the generational blessing that would begin with Abram's promised seed but would climax someday in a miracle birth of a baby born in Bethlehem. God was reminding Abram that this miracle birth would not be the last but rather the first. It would serve to remind all humanity that our hope is found in Christ alone.

Now it was time for God to change Abram's name to match his destiny. Genesis 17:5 declares, "Neither shall thy name any more be called Abram, but thy name shall be Abraham; for a father of many nations have I made thee." Abraham had asked for a son but God was going to make him a father of nations. God's plan for our lives always exceeds our dreams; for He is the God that is able to do exceedingly abundantly above what we are able to ask or think.

Why would God change Abram's name? The surface answer is quite obvious: so his name would match the destiny God had planned for his life. But the real truth goes much deeper than the obvious; for the reality is that all of us carry deep inside a mental picture of who we really are with all our flaws, failures, and limits. I call it our self-portrait, but in reality it has been painted by everyone we have come in contact with over the course of a lifetime. It is like putting a flea in a jar and screwing the lid on tightly. At first the flea jumps in hope of freedom only to experience the pain of the lid against his head. After a few attempts that resulted in the same pain, he stops jumping. Now you can remove the lid and the flea will remain in the jar. No longer is he bound by the lid but he is bound by his own thoughts. This describes all of us; we are all bound by the inner picture we have of ourselves confirmed by the pain of the past. God knew that for Abraham to experience the plan He had in mind for him, it would require a new self-portrait to be painted, reflecting not just Abraham as the father of Isaac but Abraham the father of nations. This name change would result in an identity change. Now Abraham could see himself without shame. He also could see that God was able to perform His word. The shame of the past was gone forever, the lid had been removed, the limits were gone, and Abraham was free! He was free to experience the fullness of God.

God knew that Abraham would need a sign, something to remind him that He would not change His mind concerning Abraham's future. God would seal the covenant with the act of circumcision. Though it seemed barbaric at first, upon further examination it is easy to see the meaningful truths connected to God's plan. Circumcision began with the removal of the flesh. God was subtly reminding Abraham again that this would not be a work of the flesh, but rather a supernatural work of the Spirit. In Hebrews, God would go on to remind us of our circumcision, not of hands but of the heart, as He would cut away the flesh and remove from us our ability to rest upon our own strength or religious rituals that falsely gave us hope or assurance in the past.

Secondly, circumcision put the focus on seed or reproduction, further emphasizing God's desire to reveal Himself as a generational God of Abraham, Isaac, and Jacob. God is indeed a generational God concerned not only with our personal needs but also the needs of those to follow. He wants to work in you and through you that the world may know that He is God.

Thirdly, circumcision represents intimacy and love. Our covenant is a love covenant based on His unconditional, unchanging love. We love Him because He first loved us.

Now Abraham and Sarah could rest in the love of God, knowing full well that God would fulfill their deepest longing and redeem them from their own failures. We can only imagine the joy that flooded their souls as they realized that nothing was impossible with God. But for now, there are a lot of things to do to prepare for the promise to be fulfilled. After all, preparation is the key to receiving from God. They wondered with excitement what tomorrow would bring.

Chapter Eight

Abraham the Intercessor

Genesis 18:27-"And Abraham answered and said, Behold now, I have taken upon me to speak unto the Lord, which am but dust and ashes:"

The heat of the noonday sun seemed to win out over Abraham as he sat there in the doorway of his tent. He recounted the events of late, no doubt still a bit overwhelmed by the visit that he had received recently from the Lord. He was adjusting to his new name and then still wondering how these promises will come to pass. Everything seemed impossible, but the Lord had reappeared to affirm His covenant with Abraham and to remind him of the promises made, promises that only God could perform now since both Abraham and Sarah were well past child bearing days. Even the thought of such a thing brought laughter to their hearts and a grin to their faces.

It was approaching lunchtime. Little did they know that they would be entertaining guests at this meal. Then suddenly He appeared. As Abraham looked from the ground, there before his eyes stood the Lord and with Him were three angels. He jumped to his feet and rushed out to greet them as he wondered, "What could be the purpose of this visit so close on the heels of the other?" One thing was certain in Abraham's mind: there was a purpose but this was much too holy of a moment to question. In time, His purpose would be revealed but for now, Abraham felt a need to welcome his guests and instruct his servants to kill a young calf and prepare a meal. At the same time, he ran to fetch some water to wash their feet, a custom practiced throughout history to welcome guests and refresh them from their long journey.

As they ate their meal together, the silence was deafening. Would Abraham ever know what this journey was about or would he be left to wonder? Then the Lord's voice rang out, breaking the silence, "Where is Sarah, your wife?" "She is in the tent," Abraham quickly responded. The Lord continued, "I will return to her the time of life and she shall bear you a son." Thinking she was hidden from Him, Sarah laughed in her heart. Then a second question came from his lips, "Why did Sarah laugh?" Before Abraham could respond, a third question was uttered, "Is there anything too hard for the Lord?" Sarah emerged from the tent and attempted to deny her response only to discover that the Lord knew the secret thoughts of her heart. As she stood there defenseless, suddenly the honored guests stood to their feet; it was apparent that they were leaving. Yet the visit felt so incomplete. All they had heard this visit had already been given to them on the visit before. Abraham decided to tag along just in case there was something else the Lord wanted to tell him in private.

The Lord, sensing Abraham's hunger, said to those with Him, "Shall we keep our plan between us and hide it from our friend?" With that, he turned and looked into Abraham's eyes and told Him of His plan to destroy Sodom and Gomorrah. Abraham was stunned! As he stood there, all he could think about was Lot and his family. He recalled the last time they were together between Bethel and Hai. Abraham had encouraged Lot to accompany him to Bethel (the house of God), but Lot chose instead to return to Sodom, the very place in which he had been taken captive as a prisoner of war. Though Abraham's army had freed him from the enemies, Abraham could not make Lot's choices for him. Now Lot's choice had resulted in placing his family in jeopardy, with the impending judgment of God. Only Abraham knew what was soon to occur, but what could he do now?

As he stood there, one question after another flooded his mind. He traced every step of his journey in this walk of faith. Then suddenly, he recounted the vision of the Lord that had propelled him two thousand years into the future as he watched from heaven's box seat the last week in the life of Jesus. He had witnessed it all, from His entrance into Jerusalem on the donkey, to the last supper, to the garden of Gethsemane, to Pilate's judgment hall, to Calvary and even the resurrection. He also was privy to Jesus' times of intercession on behalf of those He loved. He had listened intently as Jesus had prayed John 17. One by one Abraham recounted the seven things Jesus had prayed for his followers; now was the time to learn how to intercede from the Great Intercessor Himself.

Jesus began in John 17:11 with the subject of unity, that his followers may become one, embracing the purpose of God. This was the very thing Abraham desired for Lot and himself, yet circumstances had divided them. It had been years since they had enjoyed the fellowship of unity. Jesus continued in verse 13 to pray for joy, a joy that would spring from within them regardless of the situation in which they found themselves. "Could there still be hope for Lot to experience the joy Abraham had discovered?" Abraham wondered as Jesus continued in intercession, praying in verse 15 for their protection, of which Lot was unaware he even needed. Little did he know he was facing the judgment of God because of the wickedness of the people with whom he had chosen to live; only God could save him now.

Again, the memory of Jesus brought Abraham back to reality as Jesus prayed for their purity in John 17:17. Jesus knew that unless they kept themselves pure, they would be destroyed from the inside out. Unfortunately, Lot had allowed the wickedness that surrounded him to infiltrate his mind, cloud his views, and affect his everyday life. He had forgotten how important it is to keep spotless and sanctified unto the purpose of God.

In verse 20, Jesus continued to pray that their lives may be fruitful, that the purpose of God may reach to the next generation. How this resonated in the heart of Abraham, knowing that Isaac was soon coming and the promise of God would affect countless thousands. Would Lot be destroyed? Would his heritage also end? What would be the answer?

But Jesus was not finished praying. Jesus prayed next for their revelation, and Abraham suddenly realized that transformation depended on revelation. People would have to know better in order to do better. Maybe that's the answer for Lot; if God would only reveal Himself to Lot. He would make the right choice to follow after God.

Suddenly Abraham recounted Jesus closing his prayer with the most important subject of all: love (verse 26). Above everything, Jesus wanted his followers to know and experience the love of God. And Jesus was willing to lay down His life that this possibility could occur.

In a flash, the whole scene ended and Abraham found himself looking toward Sodom and Gomorrah with the Lord Himself standing alongside. No doubt he wondered whether or not he should break the silence, or would the Lord change His mind on His own? Would intercession make a difference? Is there anything I can do to save Lot? Questions continued flooding his mind.

The Lord had begun this visitation with three questions: Where is Sarah? Why did Sarah laugh? Is anything too hard for the Lord? Now Abraham had some questions of his own and finally his love for Lot won out over his own fears. He asked his first question: "Will you destroy the righteous with the wicked?" There was no reply, but the Lord turned His face away from Sodom to look Abraham in the eyes. He now had His full attention. He then asked his second question: "Will not the Lord of the universe do what is right?" With each question Abraham's faith and confidence grew. Now was the time to petition the Lord on Lot's behalf. "Will you save the city for fifty righteous men?" The Lord answered, "Yes I will." But then Abraham wondered to himself whether there were fifty righteous men in Sodom or not. So he ventured on, "For forty men, would you save the city?" "Yes." "For thirty men?" "Yes." "For twenty men?" "Yes." "How far can I go?" Abraham must have thought. With fear and trembling Abraham asked one more time, "Will you save it for ten righteous men." "Yes," the Lord replied. Now the question that would always remain: Did Abraham stop too soon? Would Sodom and Gomorrah end up being destroyed because Abraham had been afraid to ask God to save it for one righteous man and his family? That answer we may never know in this life but one thing is certain: God welcomes our intercession on behalf of those we love. Lot and his family were now going to be saved because Abraham was willing to stand in the gap for him and his family!

Though no one in history had ever interceded on behalf of another, Abraham had proven that faith can make a difference in the lives of those around us. It is hard for us to imagine that mere mortals can gain the attention of the God of the universe. Thank God that His ears are still open to the cries of His people. A smile creased Abraham's face as He walked alone back to his tent realizing now that he will never, truly never, be alone again. God would forever be on his side and intercession would always play a role in setting the stage for his future. Abraham realized, as we all must, that prayer and intercession play a vital role in our walk of faith. It is true that the army of God marches forward on their knees.

Chapter Nine

The Birth of Hope

Genesis 21:2-"For Sarah conceived, and bare Abraham a son in his old age, at the set time of which God had spoken to him."

Another long, hard day surrendered to the evening shadows as the sun set on the plains of Canaan. It was a scene Abraham had witnessed thousands of times, with the daily chores behind them, the camp prepared for another night. As darkness crept across the canyon, the livestock grew silent. All was quiet with the exception of a cricket's chirp or a wolf's howl in the distance. Exhausted, everyone welcomed the thought of a good night's sleep.

As Abraham turned to kiss Sarah good night, he noticed she was already fast asleep. The flickering light of the nearby campfire caressed her face, still as beautiful as ever. Yet, it was evident that time had creased her face with wrinkles, for she is now 90. But there she was, fully pregnant. It was a sight almost impossible to comprehend-from a position of hopelessness she was carrying the seed of hope within her womb.

Abraham kissed her on her forehead, rolled over, and drifted off to sleep. Hour by hour, the darkness deepens as night tightens its grip on the plains of Canaan. Suddenly just as it had gone down minutes before, the sun peeped over the eastern mountain, each ray of sunlight dancing on the canyon floor below. The light continued its invasive search into every crack and crevice to find and dispel the darkness of the night before. Finally the heat of the morning light crossed the face of Abraham, summoning him to arise. This is the dawning of a brand new day, a day like no other, a day of destiny, a day of deliverance, a day of delight. For today the promise of hope would be born.

Abraham opened his eyes only to discover that Sarah was missing. As he turned toward the door of the tent, he noticed her walk by. Scurrying to his feet, he went out to check on her. She was in labor. Through her pain, Sarah uttered these words softly to Abraham, "Today is the day!" As if all the roosters crowed in harmony, the entire camp sprang into action. Midwives took Sarah into the tent to prepare for the birth, and duties were assigned to the servants. As excitement filled the air, Abraham found himself alone with only his thoughts to contend with; he would enter into a labor of his own. For today he would become the father of a promised child; things would never be the same. He could feel the burden of responsibility being strapped to his back while he could equally feel the frailty of his own body for he was one hundred years old. Only God could sustain him, and he must trust Him more than ever.

Like contractions in his brain, Abraham's mind bounced back and forth between his history and his destiny, as he rehearsed every event that had brought him to this moment. As minutes turned into hours, Abraham wrestled with his own mind and his own mortality, he held firmly to this thread of hope: He that had begun a good work in him was able to complete it, and that with God all things are possible.

As is the case with every new father, Abraham's thoughts turned toward his own father, Terah, who had been dead for over two decades. He remembered with clarity the journey toward Canaan that had begun with his father as the leader. No doubt he recalled the day they loaded all their possessions and left Ur of the Chaldeans. Terah, leaving behind a prosperous business making idols for a wicked land and with nothing more than a promise of God, started out toward a land flowing with milk and honey. A man, his son, and a promise of God-that seemed to be all they would ever need. But Terah died, never realizing the fulfillment of that promise; what could possibly have gone wrong?

Terah by faith began his journey to follow God, apparently with the same promise of Canaan, with the remnants of his family accompanying him. Though scripture lists Abraham first in order, in reality, most theologians agree that Abraham was actually the youngest in the family.

Haran was the oldest and Nahor the middle son. The problem seemed to occur before the journey even began. Haran died, leaving behind his only son, Lot. Haran's name translated means "the unmovable mountain." Terah was devastated as he watched Haran take his last breath. This event seemed to stagger Terah in his walk of faith. Terah's name, by the way, means "station of delay." In other words, he got stuck in the pain, stuck behind an unmovable mountain. With Terah stuck, who would now assume the leadership role for the future with the elder son dead?

The lot seemed to fall to Nahor. His wife's name, Milkah, translates "queen." He seemed destined to rule and reign in this new found land. Ironically, his name means "out of breath." A picture is being formed here. Terah is stuck and Nahor is out of breath. We see that Haran's death had an impact on him as well. How do they respond to the situation at hand? History reveals that two cities were constructed in the land known as Ur, the land of the Chaldeans. One city's name is Nahor; the second city is named Haran, obviously named for the two sons of Terah. This would serve as their only marker of inheritance. But for Abraham, God had another plan entirely. We see that he was indeed the last chance for this family to receive the promise that God had planned for them.

As this tragedy unfolds, several life principles are revealed. First, everyone has pain but not everyone has progress. Secondly, pain is intended to be a process, not a destination. Refuse to name your pain, dwell, and die there. Thirdly, pain can rob you from the purpose and plan that God has for your life. What a sad story! But it doesn't end there, for Abraham's name means "exalted father." God would redeem the entire situation by exalting Abraham to take the role of his wounded father. God would renew in him the promise He had made and call him from his father's house and kindred to follow Him to a promised land. That helps us understand better why Abraham took his nephew with him. Lot had no father now, and Abraham had no son. Maybe together they could fill the void in each other's lives. We also understand better now why Abraham could not remain in that situation with Terah and Nahor. Abraham introduces a fourth principle noteworthy for all of us to follow. As we move forward even in our pain, we will certainly encounter God. When we move toward the unmovable mountain, God will remove the unmovable situations from our lives and work the process toward our good.

Abraham's deep thoughts are interrupted by the shout of a midwife, "The baby boy is here!" Suddenly the cry of the baby is heard, a tear trickles down the face of Abraham, as tension gives way to relief and joy. Abraham rushes into the tent to Sarah's side. As he brushes back the hair from her eyes, her face radiates the emotions of her heart. With a mixture of tears and laughter, she places Isaac in the arms of his father, "His name shall be Isaac for he has indeed brought us laughter."

How surreal it must have been as everyone surrounded Isaac. Wanting just a glimpse of this promised child as hope sprang eternal in the face of a baby, revealing the fifth and final principle in a living object lesson: God will bring a renewed hope out of your pain if you will put your faith in Him and wait on His perfect timing. Your pain will ultimately end in His praise as God births hope out of your hopelessness.

The longer Abraham stood there thinking of the mercy and grace of God, the less he could control his emotions. But one thought seemed to win out over all others. God's ways are not man's ways or His thoughts man's thoughts. For as the heavens are higher above the earth, so are His ways higher than our ways and His thoughts than our thoughts. Abraham laid the baby back in Sarah's arms and stepped outside to process his feeling and get a breath of fresh air. As the evening breeze blew softly against his face, Abraham stood there looking across the plains of Canaan. He watched the sun making its decent into the horizon. Another day was coming to an end as darkness was making its presence known. Abraham realized that God allows the times of darkness and desperation to come in all our lives ultimately for His purpose.

It is in the dark times of despair that we have the opportunity to mine the silver, gold, and precious stones that we can bring back out into the light as trophies of grace. We can use these jewels to strengthen our home against the fiery trials that are sure to come. God's word declares: "[9]For we are labourers together with God: ye are God's husbandry, ye are God's building. [10]According to the grace of God which is given unto me as a wise masterbuilder, I have laid the foundation, and another buildeth thereon. But let every man take heed how he buildeth thereupon. [11]For other foundation can no man lay than that is laid, which is Jesus Christ. [12]Now if any man build upon this foundation gold, silver, precious stones, wood, hay, stubble; [13]Every man's work shall be made manifest: for the day shall declare it, because it shall be revealed by fire and the fire shall try every man's work of what sort it is." (1 Corinthians 3:9-13)

As Abraham stood there taking in this beautiful sunset, he could see Ishmael playing in the dirt in the distance. He wondered in his heart how the future would play out for both of them, as he examined his own crown jewels produced by twenty-five years of desperation. First came the crown jewel of creativity. Since dark times cause our creative juices to flow, all creations come out of desperation. Whether good or bad, all creations are birthed in the laboratory of darkness. The second crown jewel is resilience. We become stronger during the difficult times of our lives. We learn to bounce back as we discover that in our weakness, His strength is made perfect. The third crown jewel is empathy. In desperate times we learn to identify with the pain of others who have gone through the fire themselves. The final crown jewel is of a brand new reality, for God uses these times of desperation to increase our capacity to embrace a brand new level of reality with Him.

As darkness once again gripped the camp, Abraham returned to the tent only to discover that the crowds were gone. He stretched out on the bed and in the flickering of the campfire light, he noticed Sarah and Isaac were fast asleep. Exhausted from the day's event, he kissed them both and rolled over wondering to himself what tomorrow may bring. But as for now, he is content to embrace the hope of today.

Chapter Ten

The Stormy Test

Genesis 22:2-"And he said, Take now thy son, thine only son Isaac, whom thou lovest, and get thee into the land of Moriah; and offer him there for a burnt offering upon one of the mountains which I will tell thee of."

The thunder clapped as the lightning flashed across the camp, awakening everyone to the fact of an impending storm on the horizon. One clash after another continued as the battle played out in the heavens with peals of thunder followed by a light show beyond description until the atmosphere was completely charged with electricity. How long would this storm last? Only God knew! But one thing was certain: all they could do now was to batten down the camp and ride it out. Because of the invisible nature of the threat, there was no time left to plan a way of escape.

Abraham tightened down the tent flap as he huddled with his family, feeling vulnerable against the power of nature's force. The sounds were deafening, the tent popping like a whip, as the wind tested the tiny structure. The smell of rain filled the air as the storm made its way across the canyon. Rain, mixed with small hail began to beat against the tent, as the wind continued to blow in unison like a demolition team working together with one purpose in mind: to destroy Abraham's home. All he could do was to hold on to his faith in God; for God was still ultimately in control, and He would see him and his family through the storm.

The ambush of the storm finally ended. The sound of thunder could hardly be heard in the distance. The storm was over and now it was time to examine the extent of the damage. Abraham unfastened the tent door and stepped outside. He could barely see in the early morning light but it appeared that everything had survived the storm, with only a few new marks on the leather tents, as a reminder of the storm.

With the storm now behind, it was time to prepare for the festivities of today. Isaac has now been weaned. It was time to celebrate and assign to him a pedagogy (bond-slave) to train him in the ways of God, quite an important day in the life of every Jewish boy. A milestone, so to speak, it was the first step in a long journey that would continue for the next twenty-seven years.

Little did Abraham realize that the storm was nothing more than a prophetic sign of what the coming day would bring as the celebration got underway. For over the last three years, Sarah had struggled with the fact that Ishmael was taking attention away from Isaac, as Abraham divided his time between both of his sons. Coupled with this problem was the fact that Ishmael served as a constant reminder of Sarah's own failure, for in her moment of weakness she had concocted a plan to help God fulfill his will by offering Hagar, her servant, to Abraham to be a surrogate mother for the promised child, a plan that God neither designed, nor would He endorse.

As the party began, everything seemed to be going well. As everyone gathered to celebrate Isaac's development, he was the center of attention until Sarah noticed Ishmael. In an attempt to garnish some attention for himself, Ishmael began to mock Isaac. This was more than Sarah could take, as all the pent up emotions of the past seemed to erupt like a volcano, bringing the whole celebration to a halt. She calls Abraham aside and says to him, "…Abraham, cast out this bondwoman and her son: for the son of this bondwoman shall not be heir with my son, even with Isaac." (Genesis 21:10)

The stormy test had begun. Though Sarah called Ishmael the son of a bondwoman, she failed to realize that he was also Abraham's son. And the birth of Isaac had not diminished Abraham's love for Ishmael. What was he to do? His heart was crushed and every eye in the camp was awaiting his response. With tears streaming down his face, he bowed his head in prayer. Once again he found himself in a storm, trusting God alone to see him through.

Suddenly God spoke to Abraham, "Do as Sarah has commanded you and do not be grievous concerning the lad. For the son of this bond woman I will also make a great nation for he is your seed." (Paraphrased) Abraham leaned over to Sarah and said, "Agreed. I'll send them away tomorrow but let us finish the celebration for now." During the celebration, Abraham continued to wrestle with his emotions, but as the day went on, the people seemed to forget the whole incident.

As morning came, Abraham got up from a restless bed and began to prepare to obey the Lord. Feeling totally helpless, he began to pack up everything he thought Hagar and Ishmael might need for their long journey ahead. Quickly he realized that he didn't even know where they were going, much less what they would need. From this overwhelming realization emerges a principle we must all remember: When we move to obey God's Word, we must trust Him with the details. It is our job to obey; it is His responsibility to work out the details. Abraham took the provisions and gave them to Hagar. Embracing Ishmael and kissing him on the top of his head, he sent them both away. As he stood there watching them walk out of sight, he must have wondered in his heart, "Will I never see him again?" Only God knew the answer, but Abraham was left with the assurance that he had obeyed the voice of God and peace would soon return to Abraham's home. The storm was over…..or was it?

Abraham retreated to a quiet place where he could process his thoughts. Looking across the plains he saw a caravan approaching. As they drew near, he noticed it was King Abimelech and his chief captain, Phichol, coming to settle a dispute over a well that the servants of Abimelech had violently taken from Abraham's servants. The agreement was finally bartered and Abraham accompanied Abimelech back to the half-way point where a covenant was cut. The covenant required seven steps. First, there was a written agreement with both parties. Secondly, the shedding of blood was required as they cut in their wrists, allowing their blood to co-mingle as they placed them together. Their blood then dripped on the contract as well as into a cup of wine from which they both would drink. Thirdly, the sacrifice of an animal in which the animal was torn in two, illustrated that if they broke their covenant, it would result in their death. Fourthly, each would walk between the pieces in a figure eight pattern (eight being the number of new beginnings), a symbol of their pledge. The fifth step would be the exchange of possessions. Abraham gave Abimelech seven sheep as a witness that he would do good by him and not evil. Sixthly would be a fellowship meal they would enjoy together. Then the covenant would end with the planting of a tree, as a meeting place, a half-way point, a place where they could come to renew their covenant. Each part of this covenant was nothing more than a prophetic act mirroring the covenant God would establish with man through the sacrifice of His own Son, the Lamb of God, settling the dispute over man's eternal existence once and for all.

Abraham returned home, with the thoughts of this new covenant burning deep in his heart, remembering the covenant he had witnessed before, early in his journey. Abraham had no idea what the future would hold. But God had a plan for Abraham that he would soon discover step by step. "¹And it came to pass after these things, that God did tempt Abraham, and said unto him, Abraham: And he said, Behold, here I am. ²And he said, Take now thy son, thine only son, Isaac, whom thou lovest, and get thee into the land of Moriah; and offer him there for a burnt offering upon one of the mountains which I shall tell thee of." (Genesis 22:1-2) Now Abraham would have to face the greatest storm of his life. What would it take for Abraham to obey God and to pass this final exam?

First it would take total submission to God and God alone. Often we view submission as a sign of weakness, but true submission is strength under control. Secondly, Abraham would have to remain sensitive to the voice of God in spite of his emotions. Only God knew the final outcome and Abraham would only gain direction for the next step in the process by the word of the Lord. Thirdly, Abraham would need to separate himself from those around him; God and Abraham both knew that those that were with him could hinder him from totally obeying God. We must be certain about those we allow to go with us to our place of sacrifice. Fourthly, Abraham would need to set the altar and wood in order. Abraham knew *how* this was done was equal in importance to *what* was being done: God is a God of order. Fifthly, Abraham would have to learn that the cost of the sacrifice in turn reveals the value of the commitment to the covenant. The greater the covenant, the more costly the sacrifice will be. Sixthly, Abraham would learn the importance of process. True followers of God follow Him step by step, realizing that God always reserves the right to control your next step. Since the steps of the righteous man are ordered of the Lord, had Abraham ignored this principle, he would have killed Isaac on the Word from God, spoken yesterday. God is always speaking. The question remains: Are we always listening? Finally, Abraham would learn that God is Jehovah Jireh, the provider in the midst of our storm. Though your faith may be tested, your God will always be proven faithful. He will pass the test. This private time between God and Abraham would serve as a reminder to Abraham to never allow the blessing of God to replace the Blesser Himself.

Abraham returned home with Isaac by his side; they had experienced something that would forever bond their hearts together, for they had witnessed God in a way which others could only dream of. They had seen the very hand of God provide for them in their greatest time of need. They heard the voice of God speak peace to the storm in their hearts. Now they knew for certain that, regardless of what life may bring, Jehovah-Jireh would meet their needs for He is the God of the storms.

Chapter Eleven

Abraham the Example

Genesis 25:7-8-"⁷And these are the days of the years of Abraham's life which he lived, an hundred threescore and fifteen years. ⁸Then Abraham gave up the ghost, and died in a good old age, an old man, and full of years; and was gathered to his people."

What an incredible life as an ordinary man learned to walk in relationship with an extraordinary God! Only God can bless us with long life and make that life full and complete. Abraham's life goes on and on with miracle after miracle. Even after the death of Sarah, Abraham married another wife, Keturah, and had six more sons, each one a miracle in and of themselves, coming from a man now at least 140 years old.

Abraham was the first Christian recorded in scripture; he is known as the father of the faithful because he put his faith in the finished work of Jesus Christ. The most astonishing thing is the fact that this one hundred-year-Christian life was recorded hundreds of years before the law was given to Moses and over 2,000 years before the birth of Jesus Christ in Bethlehem. The questions we must consider are these: Why did God do this and is there a lesson to be learned by the timing of God in His relationship to Abraham's life? I believe the answer may be too simple for some to receive. I believe Abraham lived a life of faith before the law simply because the law, or obeying the law for that matter, has nothing whatsoever to do with how we receive our salvation. Ephesians 2:8-9 declares: "⁸For by grace are ye saved through faith; and that not of yourselves: it is the gift of God: ⁹Not of works, lest any man should boast." If the faith covenant was established before the law was given, then neither the law nor our works can take the credit. All the glory is then attributed to the finished work of Jesus Christ. For He alone deserves the glory!

Although this seems to be written in black and white, millions of people hold on to the belief that their works have something to do with their salvation. Now I am in no way denying that we should work in behalf of the Kingdom of God, nor am I saying that works are not connected to the life of a believer. What I am saying is simply this: salvation is not a result of our works but rather the opposite is true. Works are a result of our salvation. We work because we are saved and not the other way around.

Abraham's walk of faith began by accepting the sacrifice of Jesus Christ as his very own, by which a transaction as well as a transformation occurred as recorded in Genesis 15:6, "And he believed in the LORD; and he counted it to him for righteousness." His faith in Christ resulted in a change in his status. He was saved and made righteous in the sight of God through a vision 2,000 years before Calvary. We, however, stand more than 2,000 years this side of the cross looking back. But the requirement for salvation remains exactly the same; we must put our faith in the finished work of Jesus Christ as Romans 10:9-10 declares, "⁹That if thou shalt confess with thy mouth the Lord Jesus, and shalt believe in thine heart that God hath raised him from the dead, thou shalt be saved. ¹⁰For with the heart man believeth unto righteousness; and with the mouth confession is made unto salvation." Jesus became sin for us; for He was the sinless sacrifice, the perfect Lamb of God that took away the sins of the world. How then can we possibly believe we become righteous by practicing righteous act? I agree that I might not understand the depth of this beautiful transaction but I am certainly convinced it is a work of grace, which is brought about in my salvation. And I also know by experience that it is a work in my heart and it does not come about by the work of my own hands. Therefore, Proverbs 4:23 carries an extreme warning, "Guard your heart above all else, for it determines the course of your life." (NLT) Or as the King James Version states this same verse, "Keep thy heart with all diligence; for out of it are the issues of life." Every issue flows from our heart; in other words, it's not just what we do that matters but why we do what we do and what we hope to obtain.

Apostle Paul used Abraham's life of faith to challenge those of his day that believed that salvation came through human effort rather than by the Spirit of God. He also presented issues we should consider before we accept the false doctrine that salvation comes from our works versus the finished work of Jesus. May I offer these issues for your consideration?

First is the issue of glory in Romans 4:2. If you hold to the belief that salvation comes as a result of the works of your hand, to whom then shall we assign the glory? If salvation is by grace through faith, then all the glory belongs to Jesus. But surely you are not suggesting that we assign the glory that belongs to God to you, a mere human being.

The second issue follows in verse 3: faith. If you believe salvation comes by result of your work, then your faith clearly is vested in your own ability, which, by the way, is limited at best. My faith is firmly planted in the finished work of Jesus which has unlimited power to save to the uttermost.

The third issue follows in verse 4: reward. If salvation is the result of the works of your hand, then you must also accept the responsibility of the rewards. In other words, you must reward yourself for a job well done. But if your faith is in Jesus, He becomes responsible for rewarding you for your works after you've experienced salvation.

Issue four is found in verse 4b: grace. Grace is defined both as unmerited favor and divine enablement. If you believe salvation is a result of human effort, then you must also reject His grace and refuse the intervention of God in your everyday life. But to the believer, grace is translated: **G**od's **R**iches **A**t **C**hrist's **E**xpense. We are therefore open to both favor and enablement from God as we walk out our relationship with Christ on a daily basis.

Issue five is the issue of righteousness which means right standing with God. If you hold to the belief that salvation is a result of works, then you must in turn reject the message of reconciliation. 2 Corinthians 5:19 declares, "For God was in Christ, reconciling the world to himself, no longer counting people's sins against them. And he gave us this wonderful message of reconciliation" (NLT) You then must set the terms of agreement for both God and you. That is precisely why those that believe in salvation by works cannot seem to come to a place of agreement on what it takes to please God. The rules are constantly changing and their lives totally inconsistent. Yet in Romans 4:6, Paul refers to David's witness of Abraham concluding "…unto whom God imputeth righteousness without works."

Issue six is contained in verse 10: the reckoning issue. Reckoning is a form of reconciliation meaning to come into agreement with Christ. Paul uses this term often. We must reckon ourselves dead to sin. We must reckon ourselves alive. We must reckon ourselves righteous. We must reckon ourselves children of our faithful father, Abraham. If we hold to our belief of salvation by works, we are left to agree only with ourselves and those we can persuade to agree with us on this dangerous doctrine.

Issue seven is the promise issue. The promise is explained in verse 13, "For the promise, that he should be the heir of the world, was not to Abraham, or to his seed, through the law, but through the righteousness of faith." To reject the idea that salvation comes as a result of faith and to cling to the belief that salvation is a result of our works excludes a person from the promise of Abraham and to rob their seed from an inheritance. There remains therefore no promise for you or your seed or as verse 14 so clearly states: "For if they which are of the law be heirs, faith is made void, and the promise made of none effect:"

Issue eight is the wrath issue. Verse 15 says, "Because the law worketh wrath: for where no law is, there is no transgression." The law was not given with the intent to make us righteous but rather to prove us guilty and subject to the wrath of God. How shall we escape the wrath of God if we seek to obtain salvation through the law and good works? Our only way to escape wrath is to run to the cross of Jesus Christ where the wrath of God has already fallen. It's like being caught in a forest fire-your only hope of safety is to find the place that has already been burned and you will escape the fire to come.

Issue nine is the father issue. Verses 16-17 tell us that God called Abraham to be the father of the faithful and a father of many nations. We know today that Abraham is recognized as the father of the Jews, a father of Muslims, and the father of the faithful or the Christian. But if you hold to the belief that salvation comes as a result of the works of your hands, then who, may I ask, is your father? What is your connection to the Heavenly Father Himself if you reject the finished work of Jesus and Abraham, His chosen vessel?

I suppose issue ten troubles me most of all; it is the issue of resurrection. Verses 23-25 close out this discussion with this conclusion, "²³Now it was not written for his sake alone, that it was imputed to him; ²⁴But for us also, to whom it shall be imputed, if we believe on him that raised up Jesus our Lord from the dead; ²⁵Who was delivered for our offences, and was raised again for our justification." Our resurrection depends entirely on the fact of whether or not we believe and accept the finished work of Jesus as being adequate to grant us righteous, declare us justified and therefore, present us before the Father blameless. If we still hold to the belief that salvation is a result of the works of our own hand, we are in turn saying that the finished work of Jesus Christ was inadequate for the task and I, in turn, must make up the difference through my works in the areas that Jesus failed. I know these are strong statements to make but this, my friend, is a serious matter. In fact, it is more than a life and death matter; it is an eternal matter that can rob you from the purpose and plan that God has for your life and destiny.

My earnest prayer and desire for you is that you consider these issues before you embrace the concept of salvation by works. And if you find yourself already a part of a group that embraces the works doctrine, that you will make a clean break with them today and accept Jesus Christ as your Lord and Savior. I pray that you may once and for all settle the issues of glory, faith, rewards, grace, righteousness, reckoning, promise, wrath, fatherhood and resurrection which are all found in the one, and only one, Savior this world will ever know, Jesus Christ, the Son of the living God.

As Peter and John declared in Acts 4:12, "Neither is there salvation in any other: for there is none other name under heaven given among men, whereby we must be saved." And if this is not evidence enough, consider the words of Jesus Himself in John 14:6, "Jesus saith unto him, I am the way, the truth, and the life: no man cometh unto the Father, but by me." Not only should we follow Abraham's example but we ourselves should become an example of faith that others can follow all the way to the cross.

Chapter Twelve

Abraham's Blessing

*Galatians 3:26-29-"²⁶For ye are all the children of God by faith
in Christ Jesus. ²⁷For as many of you as have been baptized into
Christ have put on Christ. ²⁸There is neither Jew nor Greek, there
is neither bond nor free, there is neither male nor female: for ye
are all one in Christ Jesus. ²⁹And if ye be Christ's, then are ye
Abraham's seed, and heirs according to the promise."*

This promise Apostle Paul refers to goes all the way back to Abraham's
first encounter with God in Genesis, chapter 12 which I covered in the
opening chapter of this book. This promise is multi-faceted including
direction, companionship, posterity, significance, protection, blessing, and
finally, generational impact. We have also come to see that God has been
faithful to fulfill every promise made to Abraham over four thousand years
ago. The great news for us is the fact that the blessing of Abraham did
not die when Abraham died; it remains available for the seed of Abraham
which is, in fact, every person that puts his faith firmly in the God of
Abraham through accepting Jesus Christ as Lord and Savior. Apostle Paul,
under the inspiration of the Holy Spirit goes through the process in great
detail to guide us into the fullness of Abraham's blessing.

It all comes back to our faith in the finished work of Jesus Christ as
I presented in detail in the last chapter. Hebrews 11:6 declares, "But
without faith it is impossible to please him: for he that cometh to God
must believe that he is, and that he is a rewarder of them that diligently
seek him." It is not faith in our faith but rather through faith in God that
we start the process of accessing Abraham's blessing. Yes, there will be

hurdles we must jump and a process of maturity we must go through but we, like Abraham, will come to the conclusion that the destination is well worth every step of the journey. But where do we begin?

"[3]Jesus answered and said unto him, Verily, verily, I say unto thee, except a man be born again, he cannot see the kingdom of God. [4]Nicodemus saith unto him, How can a man be born when he is old? Can he enter the second time into his mother's womb, and be born? [5]Jesus answered, Verily, verily, I say unto thee, except a man be born of water and of the Spirit, he cannot enter into the kingdom of God." (John 3:3-5) It all begins with the new birth which comes by placing our faith in Jesus Christ as our Lord and Savior or as Paul states it in Galatians 3:26, "For ye are all the children of God by faith in Christ Jesus." In our present world, we often hear the words that we are all (meaning the entire world) children of God, but that is just simply not true according to scripture. Yes, we are all the creation of God, but we only become a child of God when our faith rests in the finished work of Christ.

The second step according to Paul follows immediately in verse 27, "For as many of you as have been baptized into Christ have put on Christ." Many Christians hold to the view that "baptized into Christ" in this scripture is referring to the act of water baptism. Let me state that I emphatically believe that all new believers should indeed be baptized in water after they accept Christ as their Savior. In fact, Jesus, Himself, instructed us to do so as an outward demonstration of our inward faith. But I hold to the view that the particular baptism mentioned here is not a baptism by water, but rather one of blood. The Holy Spirit baptizes us in the blood of Christ Himself, making us a part of the family of God; for we are saved by blood, not water. After that we are to follow the Lord in water baptism as an outward confession of an inward experience. But regardless of your view, this should not stand as a point of contention in our Christian life.

Paul then goes on to use the term that we must *put on Christ*. Wow, what a statement! Putting on Christ means that we must replace the attributes of this old man, now dead and buried with Christ in baptism, with the attributes of Jesus Himself, who is now alive in our hearts. At first, most new Christians try, without success I might add, to carry out this statement through human strength and effort. In other words, we try to live for Jesus! But may I remind you that Jesus is not a dead historical figure of the past; Jesus is alive and He is now alive in your heart, by the presence of the Holy Spirit dwelling within. The victorious Christian life is not a result of you living for Christ but rather allowing the living Lord Jesus Christ to live through you in your everyday life. After all, Jesus is the only one that has ever lived a victorious Christian life to begin with, and to think we can accomplish this command without Him is nothing short of ludicrous.

As we walk out this process of allowing Christ to set the agenda for our lives, we will soon discover what He will allow and what He will not allow. One of the first things Paul speaks of in verse 28 is, "There is neither Jew nor Greek, there is neither bond nor free, there is neither male nor female: for ye are all one in Christ Jesus." Jesus will not allow us as believers to value or devalue other humans on the basis of their ethnicity, their social status, or their gender. In the flesh we use these biases to devalue and categorize people into an invisible caste system. We then only give our time, our talent and our treasure to those we deem worthy of our investment.

Jesus sought to destroy this idea during His earthly ministry as He reached out both to the elite and the outcast, to the Gentiles and the Jews, to men and, yes, to women and children alike. In fact, it was His unconditional love toward all people that caused the elite of the day to seek for a way to kill Him, lest they lose their position. You, too, will encounter adversity from those that consider themselves to be great when you attempt to treat all people equally regardless of their gender, their position, or the color of their skin. But Jesus came with one purpose in mind: to make us all one family in spite of our kindred, tribe, or tongue.

Paul explains why in Galatians 3:29, "And if ye be Christ's, then are ye Abraham's seed, and heirs according to the promise." Salvation qualifies us to inherit all that the family possesses. By accepting Christ as our personal Lord and Savior, we trade in the tribal blood that separated us through sin and works of the flesh for the precious pure blood of the Son of the living God. We receive a blood transfusion, so to speak, causing us to become a part of a royal family because we share His royal blood. Therefore, all the wealth of the Kingdom becomes ours because we are now identified as a member of the family; we are Abraham's seed now and heirs according to all that he was promised, all through the shed blood of Jesus Christ.

Paul goes on in chapter 4, verses 1-7 to explain the process we must go through as we prepare to rule and reign with Christ in the new Kingdom. As often the case, the actual process was practiced by the Jewish culture in their everyday lives; yet they failed to recognize once again that it was only a type and shadow to things to come. Everything pointed to Jesus and His Kingdom and not just their nation. One such example is the pedagogy system by which they educated their children to assume the family business.

Galatians, chapter 4 opens with this verse but it is actually a continuation of thought from the previous chapter as we walk out our new position as Abraham's seed, "[1]Now I say, That the heir, as long as he is a child, differeth nothing from a servant, though he be lord of all; [2]But is under tutors and governors until the time appointed of the father." In these two verses Paul uses four titles, fully understood by the people of that day but somewhat confusing to those of us who are stranger to the pedagogy system. They are heir, child, servant, and lord. He will introduce another title in verse seven, son, a title reserved for those that have completed the process.

A Jewish child's education began at birth and would last for thirty years with three distinct points at which success could be measured. The first three years, the child stage, would be spent with his mother as she nursed him and cared for his every need. She would also teach him their history through what we may refer to as Bible stories, but to them, it was a part of their rich history as a nation. In scripture, we find the title, male child, to describe the birth of a baby boy.

At age three, he was weaned and ready to enter the next stage. He then received a tutor or a bond slave to walk with him throughout the next twenty-seven years of the process. The child would then be dressed like one of the servants except that a purple thread was placed in the hem of his tunic, indicating that he would one day be the lord and master of the house.

It was the pedagogy or bond slave's duty to prepare this child for school. He was to teach him the Hebrew alphabet and the corresponding number since the Hebrew language can be recognized by either the letter or number. How he did this was quite unique. He would dip his finger in honey and touch it to the child's tongue as he said to him, "What you are about to learn is sweeter than the honey in the honeycomb." The same words were quoted by King David to explain the word of God all the way back in Psalm 19:10, "More to be desired are they than gold, yea, than much fine gold: sweeter also than honey and the honeycomb." Each day this process would be reiterated. Finally the child could make a connection between the sweetness of the honey and the sweetness of the Word of God.

At age five, both the child and the servant went to the Hebrew school where the teacher would have the children to dip their own fingers in honey and lick it off before the classes would begin, reciting this same phrase, "What you are about to receive is the Word of the living God, and it is sweeter than the honey in the honeycomb." The children would learn during the day and at night the pedagogy would go over all that was taught in class until it became part of the child's memory. This continued day after day until the child was around nine years old. By then he had learned and memorized twenty-four books of the Jewish law. Now it was time for the father to spend his time with the child as over the next three years he taught the child the oral law. Much too holy to write down, it could only be shared from the mouth of the father to the ear of the child. The first stage was completed when the child was around twelve years old and his Bar Mitzvah was held.

The pedagogy would bring the child before the father at the time set by the father. There he would stand and quote from memory the written and oral law of God. Upon the completion of this recital, the father would remove the clothing of the servant and replace it with his own robe, ring, and shoes representing the father's identity, authority and destiny. No longer would he be called a male child, but rather a son. This reflects the first step in our Christian walk; we must learn the word of God for ourselves.

Now the child entered a second stage. Over the next five years he was required to debate the law with the religious scholars of the day. We see

Jesus Himself doing this very thing in the temple when he was just twelve years old and the scholars were astonished at His wisdom. The purpose for this stage is that they may settle what they had learned in their own hearts. The same is true for us as believers; we must not only learn the Word of God for ourselves, we must then settle what we have learned in our hearts. The Word must become a part of our lives by settling it in our hearts.

Lastly was the third stage. Over the next thirteen years sons were required to work with their fathers in the family trade for three hours a day while they continued to study for nine hours each day. Why? That the Word of God they had learned and settled might be lived out in the workplace of their everyday lives as they assumed the family business, representing both God and the father in all the family affairs. That's why Jesus began his ministry at age thirty, in full vigor, ready to represent the Father in every area of His life. We too must learn what we believe and why we believe it, and then live out the Word of God in our everyday lives realizing that we are no longer representing ourselves, but our Father in heaven. We are in training for reigning not only in this life, but ruling and reigning with Him throughout eternity.

I would like to close this book with an invitation to join Abraham as well as all of us that consider ourselves the seed of Abraham by beginning your journey today. If you have already accepted Christ Jesus as your Lord and Savior, hopefully you will be able to identify the next step you must take in your journey. But if you however have never accepted Christ, may I introduce you to Him now as you repeat this prayer with me: *"Father God, I accept Your Son, Jesus Christ, as my personal Lord and Savior. I realize and accept His birth, His life, His death, and His resurrection as my very own. For You said in Your Word that if I confess with my mouth the Lord Jesus and believe in my heart that You raised Jesus from the dead that I would be saved. I do that right now. I invite Jesus to come into my heart. Forgive me of my sins. Thank you, Lord, for saving me. Amen."*

Welcome to the family of God! May I encourage you to read your Bible and begin talking to God daily about everything that concerns you, knowing fully that He cares. Most of all, may I encourage you to enjoy every step of the process you will go through as you learn to walk with God on this journey of faith. Happy traveling!

ABOUT THE AUTHOR

Rick Clendenen was born into a large family in a mining town in Eastern Kentucky and quickly learned the importance of friends. Not until he came to accept Jesus Christ as Lord and Savior at the age of seventeen did he find out the meaning of true friendship. Through hours of study and prayer, Rick has included many principles he has learned about the man Abraham, the one that God Himself calls His friend.

Rick accepted the call to the ministry in 1974. He and his wife Debbie have served side by side in ministry as youth leaders, assistant pastors, pastors, and many other volunteer jobs. In 2008, Rick and Debbie felt the call to organize Rick Clendenen Ministries, Inc. Through this ministry, they have been involved in church planting in India, Indonesia, Romania, South Africa, Uganda, Rwanda, and Sudan. It is their desire to see new churches planted around the world. Rick travels nationally as well conducting seminars, including training in such areas as leadership, spiritual gifts discovery, fatherhood/sonship, and the home.

Rick and Debbie have two grown children and two grandchildren. Their son Richie and wife Jenny are parents of their grandson, Trey. Their daughter Renee and husband Landon are parents of their granddaughter, Kyndal.

Rick's number one desire above all things is to simply be known as a friend of God.

Made in the USA
Monee, IL
15 July 2020